Cowley Publications is a ministry of the brothers of the Society of Saint John the Evangelist, a monastic order in the Episcopal Church. Our mission is to provide books and resources for those seeking spiritual and theological formation. Cowley Publications is committed to developing a new generation of writers and teachers who will encourage people to think and pray in new ways about spirituality, reconciliation, and the future.

T0119845

# MANY SERVANTS

## AN INTRODUCTION TO DEACONS

### REVISED EDITION

Ormonde Plater

A COWLEY PUBLICATIONS BOOK

*Lanham, Chicago, New York, Toronto, and Plymouth, UK*

A COWLEY PUBLICATIONS BOOK

ROWMAN & LITTLEFIELD PUBLISHERS, INC.

Published in the United States of America
by Rowman & Littlefield Publishers, Inc.
A wholly owned subsidiary of
The Rowman & Littlefield Publishing Group, Inc.
4501 Forbes Boulevard, Suite 200, Lanham, Maryland 20706
www.rowmanlittlefield.com

Estover Road, Plymouth PL6 7PY
United Kingdom

Copyright © 2004 by Ormonde Plater
First Rowman & Littlefield edition 2009

Scripture quotations are taken from *The New Revised Standard Version* of the
Bible, © 1989, by the Division of Christian Education of the National Council
of the Churches of Christ in the United States of America. Used by
permission.

*All rights reserved.* No part of this publication may be reproduced, stored in a
retrieval system, or transmitted in any form or by any means, electronic,
mechanical, photocopying, recording, or otherwise, without the prior
permission of the publisher.

British Library Cataloguing in Publication Information Available

**Library of Congress Cataloging-in-Publication Data**

Plater, Ormonde.
    Many servants : an introduction to deacons / Ormonde Plater.—Rev. ed.
        p. cm.
    Includes bibliographical references and index.
    978-1-56101-270-1 (pbk. : alk. paper)
    1. Deacons.  I. Title.
    BV680.P55 2004
    262'.14—dc22                                          2004018750

Printed in the United States of America.

☉™ The paper used in this publication meets the minimum requirements of
American National Standard for Information Sciences—Permanence of
Paper for Printed Library Materials, ANSI/NISO Z39.48-1992.

# CONTENTS

## PREFACE TO THE REVISED EDITION

✳

First published in 1991, this book was printed three times before going out of print. Along the way, it proved useful, educational, and even inspirational to many deacons, persons in discernment, candidates in formation, and others curious about deacons.

After more than a dozen years, the time has come for a second edition. The meaning and functions of deacons have evolved, the order has grown in numbers and importance, new canons governing diaconal ministry have been enacted, and new issues are affecting the practice of the diaconate. Above all, deacons have stories to tell, defining their role in God's plan, and I have let them speak with little editorial interference. I have also added a calendar of deacon saints, compiled from several sources over the past decade. All this has resulted in a book in many ways original. Some parts I have kept, some altered, some put away, some added.

During revision I shared the draft manuscript with the current class of deacon candidates in the Diocese of Louisiana, and I thank one of them, Lydia Hopkins, for her close reading and many helpful comments.

Quotations from the Bible are from the New Revised Standard Version, and quotations of psalms are from the Book of Common Prayer of the Episcopal Church.

✳

This book is my attempt to tell the story of the deacons of the church. Among many forms of religious renewal in the last two generations, Christian churches have experienced the recovery of the order of deacons after centuries of neglect and misuse. Once perceived as partially formed clerics growing toward the complete priesthood, or as purely liturgical assistants, deacons now appear in a mature role as persons specifically chosen and committed for life to ordained ministry. Although this book is mainly about the deacons of the Episcopal Church, the renewal of the diaconate plays an important role in the Canadian and other Anglican churches, in the Roman Catholic Church, in Lutheran and Reformed churches, in Orthodoxy, and in ecumenical endeavors at the national and international levels.

✳

In all churches that have recovered the diaconate, the work has involved efforts to determine the meaning and functions of the order, and its relationship to other orders and forms of ministry, based on its origins, unfolding, and evolution in the early church and its re-emergence in recent times. In this recovery no motivation has been more influential than the biblical models of *agape* and *diakonia*. Both *agape* (divine love) and *diakonia* (sacred agency) are linked to charity or care of the needy, derived from the ancient responsibility of all Jews and Christians to serve other persons and fortified by the urgent need for such service in our own age. A significant interest in social care arose in Europe in the early nineteenth century, a continent afflicted by war, poverty, and social upheaval, and continued into the turbulent twentieth century. In our time, in a world even more devastated and unstable, one attribute of all Christian churches has been a concern to care for the needs of the world outside. Churches that once served mainly their own members have learned again to serve others. In every diocese and every congregation—through church, ecumenical, and secular organizations, as members of groups and as individuals, at work and at home—Christians reach out to those in need. In this renewal they bring to life an ancient Hebrew and Christian tradition: mercy, peace, and justice for the poor of Yahweh and Jesus.

Since about 1980, the work of deacons in the Episcopal Church has become closely identified with the baptismal ministry of ordinary Christian people who reach out to the poor, sick, and oppressed. Although care of the needy thus became established as an essential ministry of deacons, attempts to restore the order have caused controversy, debate, and resistance in some places. If care of the poor is the common obligation of every Christian, why bother to ordain deacons to do this same work? It is not enough, apparently, to appeal to the Bible and ancient tradition for the meaning and role of the order, or to point out that the liturgy of the church includes deacons as a full and equal order. Attempts to answer questions about the necessity of a real and vibrant diaconate have involved two main approaches, both based on the diaconate as it existed in the early church. First, as distinct symbols of Christ the Servant, deacons function among the faithful as special models of common Christian service who lead, enable, and encourage other Christians in charitable service. Second, the functions of deacons extend beyond the ordinary charitable work of all Christians into areas where official sanction, lifelong commitment, and sacramental grace strengthen the activity of the church. Many deacons serve in administrative positions, often within the diocesan structure, and deacons in general take seriously the bishop's command at their ordination to interpret the world to the church.

These two approaches are not without their own problems. One is the ambiguous meaning of symbol in the world today. In earlier centuries the symbols or sacramental signs of the church, including its ordained ministry, were supposed to be elevated, distant, often inaccessible, and clearly defined. Although this attitude has not entirely disappeared, we now live in a society in which many people prize function for its practicality and disparage symbols for their inefficiency, playfulness, and uncertain effect. To paraphrase Flannery O'Connor (who was defending the Eucharist at a dinner party), if it's just a symbol, to hell with it! In this mentality ministry has become reduced to the performance of necessary ecclesial tasks, for which ordination is less an essential than is training and competency. Since priests and other baptized persons between them can perform all the liturgical, pastoral, and charitable tasks of deacons, a diaconate defined in terms of symbol makes little practical sense to many persons. Moreover, the diaconate appears to complicate, and to clutter with additional clericalism, a church that is trying to restore the ministry of all the baptized.

All ministry in the church—not just ordained—appears headed for drastic change and an unpredictable future in what is commonly called "the millennium of the laity." This is especially true of the diaconate, which tends to avoid not only a fixed definition but also a fixed place in the church. Deacons explore their origins, try new directions, and test the limits of their ministry. They like to speak of themselves as occupying some vague space between church and world, or between clergy and laity, as a bridge or as dancers on a razor's edge, whereas many others in the leadership of the church prefer to cling to established roles with distinct duties and responsibilities. Those who prefer simple meanings, rigid structures, and clear answers will not find them in the modern diaconate, which seems always in the process of becoming something else with elusive meanings and shifting functions. Dioceses and congregations that encourage deacons to evolve and change in their ministry, and that give free rein to local imagination and creativity, have the least difficulty with problems of definition and role.

Another problem concerns a fundamental contradiction in the way the church uses the order. To renew the diaconate, we have had to take a medieval practice—the deacon as temporary intern for priest—and alongside it reestablish an ancient practice—the deacon as permanent agent of the church. The two forms of the diaconate, ancient and medieval, carry the same name and are entered through the same ordination rite, but they are by no means equivalent, and they coexist in an uneasy parallel. The restoration of the ancient practice of the diaconate has resulted in differences between deacons and priests (including deacons on the way to the priesthood) in status, lifestyle, and ministry. As with all reforms, these distinctions have produced confusion, anger, and resistance—among lay persons who view deacons as a threat to their baptismal ministry, among priests who cherish the diaconate through which they once passed, and even among those few deacons who identify themselves closely with the priesthood. The restoration of the diaconate challenges the church to find new ways of expressing the ancient bond between deacons and bishops, and to develop a healthy relationship among deacons, priests, and other Christian ministers based on a theology of mutual and distinct ministry, not on practices that nourish disorder and competition.

Even in places where the order has been successfully restored, it tends to evolve in unexpected ways, creating new and often surprising forms of an ancient order. Changes in the diaconate tend to change the church. Ultimately, the only answer to the problem of change is to allow the change to take place, to observe what happens, and to share the story.

Deacons have a strong awareness of their historic role as go-between or herald, carrying words and deeds from one place to another. Recent scholarly studies challenge the popular translation of the Greek word *diakonia* and its cognates, including *diakonos*, as "service" in the sense of care of the needy and even menial labor. An Orthodox bishop and theologian, Paulos Mar Gregorios, argues that *diakonia* involves not only mercy, justice, and prophecy, but also worship, upbuilding the church, royal priesthood, and prayer and intercession.[1] This broadening of definition is reflected (although with different findings) in the writings of John N. Collins. In his study of hundreds of *diakon-* words used in Greek writings from the late fifth century before Christ to the fourth century of the Christian era, Collins finds that ancient sources fail to support the linguistic assumptions many make when they speak of baptized "servants" in a "servant church" and of deacons as particular "servants." The interpretation of *diakon-* words as referring solely to social care appears to date from the early nineteenth century, when German Lutherans sought to recover the original ministry of deacons and deaconesses as servants of the poor, the sick, neglected children, and prisoners. The interpretation survived, flourished, was recorded in German theological dictionaries in the 1930s, and after World War II surfaced in Germany as part of the rationale for the establishment of the permanent diaconate by the Roman Catholic Church. Along the way, it influenced the understanding of *diakonia*—now usually translated "service" instead of "ministry"—and the restoration of the diaconate in Anglican and other churches.

When early Christians called someone "deacon," though, they had more in mind than the service that all Christians are obliged to perform. Collins finds remarkable consistency among pagan, Jewish, and Christian writers of the ancient Greek world, who tended to use words of *diakonia* and its cognates in three related and often overlapping groups of meaning.

First, they used these terms in the sense of "message," to talk about a go-between, mouthpiece, or courier, who travels from one place to another and conveys goods, who carries messages on behalf of persons in high places (sometimes from a god to mortals, and vice versa), who bears the sacred word as a herald, who interprets the words of others, who intervenes on an important mission, who mediates through writing, and who even stirs the emotions of an audience through song.

Second, they used these terms in the sense of "agency," to talk about an agent, instrument, or medium who conducts an operation, acts on behalf of others, carries out the desires or commands of a superior, implements another's plan, performs civic duties and undertakings, who gets done whatever needs to be done, and who functions within the social system like a tutor, butler, major domo, personal secretary, or other important factotum.

Third, they used these terms in the sense of "attendance," to talk about one who attends to a person or household, waits on others, fetches objects and persons, cares for the needs of a guest, and on formal and hence religious occasions bears the wine cup and conducts the feast with decency and taste.[2]

Early Christian writers used *diakon-* words, including eighty places in the New Testament, to talk about Jesus, themselves, and others as spokespersons and emissaries of heaven, emissaries in the church, and others who exercise commissions within Christian communities to act under God, the church, and the Spirit. When early Christians wrote of a "deacon" of the church, they meant an agent in sacred affairs, who worked closely with the bishop, spoke for him, acted for him, and attended him. Even when the context of the agency was care of the needy, they perceived the activity as ministry to the Lord and not as ministry or service to the poor and the widows.

The design of this book, then, is to reflect on the history of deacons in the church, and to record the emerging meanings and functions of *diakonia* and deacons in the modern church and the directions in which they appear to be heading. Many dioceses of the Episcopal Church select, form, and deploy deacons. Dioceses of the Anglican Church of Canada have joined this renewal, and other churches are observing the Anglican experience for help in their own efforts. Thus another purpose of this book is to provide information and guidance for the revival of the diaconate.

The book consists of two parts. In the first, I treat scholarly and practical matters: scriptural origins, history of deacons, ecumenical spread, and selection, formation, and ministry in dioceses of the Episcopal Church. In the second, I speak about the meaning and practice of the diaconate, as revealed in the ordination liturgy, in the stories of twenty-five deacons, and in closing reflections on those stories and their significance.

Years ago the late Wesley Frensdorff, bishop of Nevada, told me about an old Yiddish curse: "May you have many servants!" The curse has in mind those servants who are lazy afflictions, who corrupt the house with lewdness and theft, and who bind their master and mistress in chains of disorder. In this book I extol the virtues of good servants, as articulate and cheerful as Figaro and Susanna, as resourceful and intelligent as Jeeves, as loyal and energetic as Bunter, as strong and enduring as Dilsey, and I argue that God will provide good servants to those who seek them and sustain them.[3] Good servants free those they serve, and many good servants free many.

XIV

CHAPTER ONE

✳

# ORIGINS

To understand deacons in the church, one must bathe deeply in two rivers flowing through the biblical landscape. In the first stream, *agape*, run the waters of God's unconditional love for human beings and of our human duty "to do justice and to love kindness" (Micah 6:8). From the second stream, *diakonia*, God sends forth human beings as emissaries on a dusty but holy mission, with orders to proclaim the good news and heal the sick. Common to both biblical themes is the concept of service, called by various names and interpreted in a variety of ways. Scripture abounds with sayings and stories about servants. In the ancient writings of the Hebrew people, commandments and prophecies lay down a strict law of mercy and justice, and in the Christian writings, which contain several references to early deacons, Jesus and his followers teach us, by word and deed, to love others and perform acts of compassion. This scriptural basis has reinforced the modern understanding of the diaconate as a sacred ministry of liturgy, word, and charity, as a sacramental representation of the deacon Christ and his diaconal church, and as part of God's ordering of the church in a divine plan of creation and salvation.[1]

## THE HEBREW SCRIPTURES

The biblical tradition of charity is older than the Torah, older even than the Hebrew people, and broader in ethnic scope. The desire to help the oppressed and dispossessed is primitive and widespread, a natural tendency in the human race. Over countless ages human beings have inherited and absorbed the practice of caring for others. By the design of God we are born to care, with good fortune we learn care in the hospitality of our first home, and at our best we hand over care to the young, who do the same in their turn. Our inclination to love God and each other comes from our nature as creatures made in the image of God. In the older, Yahwist account of creation, the first activity of Adam is to till and keep the garden of Eden (Gen. 2:15). In a myth passed on by oral tradition and finally written down, Adam begins existence as a farmhand of the Lord. Even when he falls, and is sent forth from Eden, his work is "to till the ground from which he was taken" (Gen. 3:23). In the account of the great flood Noah gathers and keeps animals and feeds them (Gen. 7). He is a livestock servant, an agent of the Lord. These myths consistently place human beings in a relationship to God.

Our relationship to God inspires our relationship to our neighbor, service for the benefit of other people. A particular concern of ancient Near Eastern legal codes is relief of the suffering of the poor, widows and orphans, aliens, and the oppressed. This concern carries over into the legal collections of the Old Testament, which were descended from ancient case law. The major legal collections of the Torah or Pentateuch show consistent concern for the poor, or *anawim*, a term that includes all those in need. In all of the collections the people of God are commanded to treat the poor with charity and justice, and this concern is linked with regulations for worship.

The earliest of these is the Covenant Code (Exod. 20:2–23:19). Among its many cultic regulations and laws protecting human beings and property are prohibitions against wronging aliens, widows and orphans, the poor, and others in need (Exod. 22:21–27; 23:1–9). The central episode of Israel as the people of God includes their experience as slaves in Egypt, saved through the mercy and justice of God. Thus, when the Covenant Code forbids the listener to wrong and oppress a stranger, it adds: "you know the heart of an alien, for you were aliens in the land of Egypt" (Exod. 23:9). This refrain appears also in the later codes.

The Deuteronomic Code (Deut. 12–26), believed to be the famous scroll, or Book of the Law, "discovered" in the temple in 621 BCE, stresses justice, equity, care of the poor, and hospitality for the sojourner (or resident alien): "When you reap your harvest in your field and forget a sheaf in the field, you shall not go back to get it; it shall be left for the alien, the orphan, and the widow" (24:19).

2

❋

And the reason for the command: "Remember that you were a slave in the land of Egypt" (24:22). The law proves sensitive even to ecology: "If you come on a bird's nest, in any tree or on the ground, with fledglings or eggs, with the mother sitting on the fledglings or on the eggs, you shall not take the mother with the young" (22:6).

Finally, the Holiness Code (Lev. 17–27) contains mainly religious and cultic laws. Israel must be holy as God is holy. But in one section, chapter 19, the code groups commands that are primarily ethical, in the tradition of the Decalogue, the Covenant Code, and the Deuteronomic Code. Gleanings from fields and vineyards shall be left "for the poor and the alien" (19:10); "When an alien resides with you in your land, you shall not oppress the alien" (19:33). And again the reason: "for you were aliens in the land of Egypt" (19:34).

In all of these collections, the memory of the Exodus informs the Hebrew understanding of humanitarian needs and concerns. Yet the Hebrew experience and remembrance of salvation also include the profound knowledge that God is the source and example of mercy. Justice is the beginning and goal of ritual. Service of the poor embraces service of the Lord. Praise of God includes praise of the Lord who uplifts the poor:

> For the Lord your God is God of gods and Lord of lords,
> the great God, mighty and awesome, who is not partial
> and takes no bribes, who executes justice for the orphan
> and the widow, and who loves the strangers, providing
> them food and clothing. You shall also love the stranger,
> for you were strangers in the land of Egypt.
> (Deut. 10:17–19)

Justice for the poor persists as a major theme in other Hebrew writings. In the Song of Hannah (1 Sam. 2:1–10) she praises the Lord who "raises up the poor from the dust" and "lifts the needy from the ash heap, to make them sit with princes and inherit a seat of honor." Hannah's prayer is the model for the Song of Mary (Magnificat) in Luke; both songs speak about God's power to raise the downtrodden. Hannah prays to the Lord as his "servant" (1:11), and she conceives Samuel, consecrating him to the service of the Lord.

Justice for the *anawim* is also a prominent theme in many psalms. Whatever the tangled history of their date and authorship, the psalms, once attributed to David, represent the heart of Hebrew worship. There the God who brought Israel out of Egypt is "the helper of orphans" (Ps. 10:15), who "does not despise nor abhor the poor in their poverty" (Ps. 22:23), and who will set right the victims of crooked deeds. The law is the subject of the extended meditation of Psalm 119, in which righteousness is defined as service of the Lord according to his commandments. Another prominent theme of the psalms is praise of the Lord who helps the poor. Psalm 146 sings of God

> Who gives justice to those who are oppressed,
> and food to those who hunger.
>
> The LORD sets the prisoners free;
> the LORD opens the eyes of the blind;
> the LORD lifts up those who are bowed down.
>
> The LORD loves the righteous;
> the LORD cares for the stranger;
> he sustains the orphan and widow,
> but frustrates the way of the wicked. (Ps. 146:6–8)

This passage, important in prophetic literature, appears in slightly different form in Isaiah 61:1–2, which Jesus reads in the synagogue at Nazareth:

> The Spirit of the Lord is upon me,
> because he has anointed me
> to bring good news to the poor.
> He has sent me to proclaim release to the captives
> and recovery of sight to the blind,
> to let the oppressed go free,
> to proclaim the year of the Lord's favor. (Luke 4:18–19)

Concern for the poor is also a major message of the prophets. A prophet, a *nabi*, is also an advocate, a *goel*, who speaks for God as a voice for the voiceless. Amos, Hosea, Micah, and Isaiah attack the corruption and injustice typical of both kingdoms in the eighth century, and the prophets just before and during the exile in Babylon continue the old theme. In the Temple Sermon, Jeremiah

4

ascribes God's protection not to the presence of the temple but to the morality of the people:

> For if you truly amend your ways and your doings, if you truly act justly one with another, if you do not oppress the alien, the orphan, and the widow, or shed innocent blood in this place, and if you do not go after other gods to your own hurt, then I will dwell with you in this place, in the land that I gave of old to your ancestors forever and ever. (Jer. 7:5–7)

The temple was built to house the commandments, but the people forgot to obey the commandments, especially those to ensure justice and true worship. The great prophet of the Exile, Ezekiel, defines righteousness as individual deeds of justice. The righteous one "does not oppress anyone, but restores to the debtor his pledge, commits no robbery, gives his bread to the hungry and covers the naked with a garment, does not take advance or accrued interest" (18:7–8). Ezekiel's famous vision in which the spirit of God enters the dry bones of the exiles while sinews and flesh grow upon them (37:1–14) must be interpreted as a people restored not only to a place, but also to deeds of justice.

From the earliest legal collections to the prophetic writings after the Exile, therefore, the Hebrew scriptures are consistent in their moral teachings about care for the poor. Among the poor (*anawim*) they number all the afflicted, especially the powerless and the oppressed, the humble and meek, widows and orphans, and "strangers" (sojourners and aliens). All these categories of the poor remind the Hebrew people not only of their ancient history as slaves and outcasts, but also of their obligation to help the poor always.

Biblical references to servants are varied and often confusing in meaning. A common word in the Hebrew scriptures is the noun *'ebed*, which means servant (in a number of senses) but also household slave, child, subject of a king, and worshiper of God. In the Septuagint, the Hebrew scriptures of Hellenistic Jews and Christians, *'ebed* is never translated *diakonos* (minister or servant) but *doulos* (slave) or *pais* (child). Although many early Christians appear to have emphasized the latter meanings, the most common interpretation today is servant. Of all the many meanings of this term and its cognates, however, its cultic or liturgical aspect has been the most neglected. The purpose of the exodus from Egypt is not solely freedom from slavery, for God saves the people of Israel out of Egypt to render 'abodah, or worshipful service, to Yahweh. This is the context, a fundamental affinity with God, in which servants perform compassion. Out of their sacrifices of blood and incense, of praise and thanksgiving, flow works of mercy and justice.

Most uses of 'ebed involve a common or ordinary use of servant imagery, applied to God's creation, to men and women made in the image of God, and to God's chosen people. But there is also a specific, theologically heightened dimension—the 'ebed Yahweh, or servant of the Lord. The 'ebed Yahweh is a specially designated person, a servant of the Lord but also united with the Lord, carrying out God's commandments and God's plan of creation and salvation. In the Hebrew scriptures this servant acts as divine agent principally in the prophecies of Second Isaiah (Isa. 40–55), and, most important, in the great Servant Songs, written in joyful hope of the restoration from exile in Babylon. For the author of the songs, 'ebed Yahweh appears to be the nation of Israel, chosen by God, suffering in exile, ultimately faithful, and restored out of death. For Christians, Isaiah's portrayal of the suffering servant of the Lord constitutes the most explicit prophecy in the Hebrew scriptures of the incarnation, death, and resurrection of Jesus. The songs live on in the gospel when Jesus says that he came not to be served but to serve. He is God's agent, the servant whom the Lord has chosen to save the people of God. The church, the image of Christ, is the body which makes the servant of the Lord present among us, and the deacons, the servants of the church, continually remind the people of the image of the diakonos Christ.

## THE CHRISTIAN SCRIPTURES

When we turn to the New Testament, the tradition that we found in the Hebrew writings persists abundantly in the teachings and deeds of Jesus and in the stories, sayings, and writings of early Christians. The biblical tradition is commonly identified with the teaching of Christ that "whoever wishes to become great among you must be your servant, and whoever wishes to be first among you must be slave of all," and with the description of Christ as one who "came not to be served but to serve, and to give his life as a ransom for many" (Mark 10:43-45). This passage and related ones have been widely used to depict Christ as the model for the service of all baptized Christians, as well as for the deacons who serve in a special way. When the passage is taken in its entirety, however, the *diakonia* that Christ came to render becomes not care of the needy but death on the cross.

There is no question that care of the needy is a Christian imperative. When he is challenged to justify his actions on the basis of the law, Jesus summarizes and interprets the ancient legal tradition in the great commandment (Matt. 22:34-40; Mark 12:28-34; Luke 10:25-28). To the question of a Pharisee, "Teacher, which commandment in the law is the greatest?" Jesus replies:

> "You shall love the Lord your God with all your heart, and with all your soul, and with all your mind." This is the greatest and first commandment. And a second is like it: "You shall love your neighbor as yourself." On these two commandments hang all the law and the prophets. (Matt. 22:37-40)

The second commandment requires us to determine the meaning of the terms *neighbor* and *love*. Is neighbor the person who lives next door or in the same village, or just the poor and oppressed, or everybody? Luke answers the question by following the commandment with the parable of the Good Samaritan. A neighbor is someone we encounter who is helpless, who needs our mercy, and love is showing mercy to the helpless one. Of the three persons who encounter the helpless man—a priest, a Levite, and the Samaritan—only the Samaritan stops and helps. Christ asks: "Which of these three, do you think, was a neighbor to the man who fell into the hands of the robbers?" The questioner answers correctly: "The one who showed him mercy" (Luke 10:36-37). The parable contains the traditional three elements—a caring person, a poor person, and mercy and justice—and thus renders an image of the Trinity in human form.

Care of the poor and oppressed was a central feature of Jesus' ministry, alongside proclamation of the good news. In Matthew's account of the commissioning of the twelve, Jesus tells them: "As you go, proclaim the good news, 'The kingdom of heaven has come

7

near.' Cure the sick, raise the dead, cleanse the lepers, cast out demons" (Matt. 10:7–8). Charity, in the form of miracles of mercy, is a sacred activity that reveals the kingdom of heaven. Christ sends this message to John the Baptist: "the blind receive their sight, the lame walk, the lepers are cleansed, the deaf hear, the dead are raised, and the poor have good news brought to them" (Matt. 11:5, cf. Luke 7:22). Those who are healed, "the lame, the maimed, the blind, the mute," respond by giving glory to "the God of Israel" (Matt. 15:30–31). Proclamation and mercy take place in a setting of worship here and in Christ's preaching at Nazareth, where he quotes from Isaiah 61:1–2 that God "has anointed me to bring good news to the poor" (Luke 4:18).

In the teachings of Christ and the prayers and songs of his followers, we have the new revelation: the hungry hunger for the bread of life, the thirsty thirst for living water, the blind see the light of Christ and the deaf hear the good news, lepers are cleansed so that they can perform rites of praise, the dead are raised as signs of the kingdom. Jesus' most explicit teaching about the poor and oppressed in the New Testament occurs in Matthew's account of the great judgment. The passage helps to explain the nature of Christian loving service. The blessed will inherit the kingdom if they show mercy:

> For I was hungry and you gave me food,
> I was thirsty and you gave me something to drink,
> I was a stranger and you welcomed me,
> I was naked and you gave me clothing,
> I was sick and you took care of me,
> I was in prison and you visited me. (Matt. 25:35–36)

Here the symbolic meaning of the poor achieves a profound dimension. The poor are Christ, Christ is the poor. The list implies another mode of the real presence of Christ, alongside his presence in the gathered people of God, in the word proclaimed and preached, and in the bread and wine of the Eucharist. Because our encounter with the poor brings us face to face with Christ, Christian ministry is not only service to the poor but also, and mainly, service to God.

In the Greek of the New Testament what occurs between the followers of Christ and the hungry, the thirsty, the stranger, the naked, the sick, and the prisoner is called *diakonia*, which means agency, ministry, or service of several kinds, including running errands, delivering messages, and performing assigned tasks. The immediate context is table-service: "For who is greater, the one who is at table or the one who serves? Is it not the one at the table? But I am among you as one who serves" (Luke 22:27)—the Greek translates literally as "the one attending." Assuming the role of waiter, Jesus reverses convention and waits on his disciples. In a similar reversal, at the Last Supper Jesus washes the feet of his followers (John 13:1–11). Washing feet is the humble action of a slave—Jesus uses the word *doulos*—but Jesus expands slavery, the abysmal, abject, and involuntary labor of an owned-inferior for an owner-master, into a sacred act under God similar to his sacrifice on the cross. Waiting on others is a divine action as well as an ethical disposition. Christ leaves this supper and this discourse to offer himself on the cross.

Like the Hebrew word commonly translated "servant," the Greek word *diakonos* offers a variety of meanings and problems of definition. It appears to have descended from the Indo-European roots *dia*, meaning thoroughly, and *ken* (or its suffixed o-form *kono*), meaning active. Another possible etymology, popular among early Greeks, combines two Greek words meaning "through the dust," and hence *diakonoi* may have been originally "dusty ones" in the sense of hurried activity on the road. As a Greek common noun, *diakonos* came to mean a particular kind of servant on a prominent level, especially the messenger, go-between, or personal attendant who delivers the orders and carries out the desires and commands of a superior. Because early Christian deacons were heavily involved in ministry to the needy, centuries later the word evolved to mean an ordained servant of charity. This complex verbal ancestry suggests a definition important for our contemporary understanding of the deacon. A deacon is one appointed and given grace to be thoroughly active and dusty in the service of the church, which necessarily involves care of the poor. Often overlooked in studies on deacons, but pertinent to *diakonia*, is the account of Jesus sending missionaries to proclaim the good news and cure the sick. If ill-received by those at their destination, they are to shake the dust from their feet (Matt. 10:14; Luke 10:11). In Luke's version he follows this *diakonia* event with the *agape* commandment and the

Good Samaritan, another person who pursues a mission on a dusty road.

Paul sometimes uses the term *diakonos* to refer to himself and others who speak the message of God: Paul and Apollos are "*diakonoi* through whom you came to believe" (1 Cor. 3:5). Paul also uses the term *doulos*, slave or lowest form of servant, to signify a menial way of life, voluntarily chosen, referring to himself as "*doulos* of Christ" (Gal. 1:10). Far more prominent is his use of the word in the majestic hymn on the Incarnation:

> Let the same mind be in you that was in Christ Jesus, who, though he was in the form of God, did not regard equality with God something to be exploited, but emptied himself, taking the form of a slave, being born in human likeness. (Phil. 2:5–7)

In the midst of many parables and sayings about servants, two passages in the gospels have significant implications for the pastoral and sacramental life of the church. In the first passage John tells of the marriage at Cana, which is the first sign to reveal the glory of Christ ( John 2:1–11). The account includes wine-bearing servants (*diakonoi*) and a chief steward, or headwaiter. This is the imagery of a feast, and these servants are table waiters whose function is to prepare and serve the wine. Obeying an order from an unexpected source, the mother of Jesus, they become agents and witnesses of the transformation of water into wine, but also of old life into new life.[2] In the second passage Jesus sends two disciples to prepare the Passover (Matt. 26:17–19; Mark 14:12–16; Luke 22:7–13). They are a model for all who prepare, and in particular they suggest the deacons and others who prepare the altar and set upon it the bread and wine of the Eucharist, our celebration of the paschal lamb.

In the grand sweep of *diakonia* and *diakonoi* that fills the New Testament, actual deacons play a tiny role. Even when deacons are mentioned, they may not exercise a formal, cultic office in the community. As we now know, the three orders did not appear full blown on the Day of Pentecost; formal offices evolved gradually, at different times and at different places, during the period in which the Christian scriptures were written and even afterwards. There is a gap in time, and yet a conceptual development, between the dea-

10
✳

cons we hear of in Paul's letters to the Philippians and Romans (probably written in the 50s), and the deacons of Acts (after CE 70) and 1 Timothy (near the end of the first century). When deacons are mentioned, usually they are linked with bishops, indicating a direct and personal association.

In the salutation of his letter to the Philippians, Paul greets the *episkopoi kai diakonoi*, who, despite the usual translation "bishops and deacons," may be simply "overseers and agents." In Paul's list of gifts exercised for the good of the community (Rom. 12:6–8), several gifts suggest roles associated with deacons from early times; the term *diakonia* (in NRSV translated "ministering," in RSV "serving") refers to delivering the word of God. The issue of women as deacons is raised in Romans 16, where Paul winds up his letter by commending to his readers in Rome "our sister Phoebe, a deacon [*diakonon*] of the church at Cenchreae, so that you may welcome her in the Lord as is fitting for the saints, and help her in whatever she may require from you, for she has been a benefactor of many and of myself as well" (16:1–2). Phoebe may be a church emissary in the informal sense, or she may be a formal deacon. When she travels to Rome with Paul's letter, however, she functions in the diaconal role of a messenger or ambassador acting under the direction of a church leader.[3]

The later writings refer clearly to a specific office, and by the last third of the first century we can speak with assurance of deacons in the church. In Acts 6:1–6 Luke does not use the word *diakonos* for the seven men appointed "to wait on tables," and the passage thus cannot be said to speak of historical deacons. But he does use words related to diaconal work:

> Now during those days when the disciples were increasing in number, the Hellenists complained against the Hebrews because their widows were neglected in the daily distribution [*diakonia*] of food. And the twelve called together the whole community of the disciples and said, "It is not right that we should neglect the word of God in order to wait on [*diakonein*] tables." [Acts 6:1–2]

A *diakonia* of tables probably refers to serving the word of God, instead of, or as well as, serving food. The preferred work of the apostles is similarly described as prayer and "serving [*diakonia*]

11
✳

the word" (6:4). Luke's intention appears not to record the first ordination of deacons in the infant church but, using a past event in conscious anticipation, to comment on *diakonia* and the related ministries of bishops and deacons in his own time.[4]

The passage offers guidance in our time also. It tells us that the community bestows orders for ministry at the direction of its leaders, and that the selection is a simple, brief process in which the community chooses the best of many, those "of good standing, full of the Spirit and of wisdom" (6:3). The community discerns those who have gifts, *charismata*, from God. Prior qualification as a faithful and prudent Christian is more important than competency or training for specific tasks—which are not even mentioned. The appointment, or ordering, consists of a prayer together with the laying on of hands by those who preside, which represents solidarity among those who perform *diakonia*, or commissioned duties, in the community. Their deployment is diverse; although originally chosen for ministry at the tables of Greek-speaking widows, a public function under the direction of the apostles, Stephen goes on to preaching and martyrdom, while Philip spreads the good news and baptizes. It is important to recognize that the community does not ordain simply to fill an occasional need; in the long run the daily ministerial structure of the community, for the purpose of mission, is more important than discrete diaconal "jobs."

In 1 Timothy 3:8–13, a list of qualifications for deacons, reflecting a church that is struggling to organize itself, also offers guidance for our time. First, the passage occurs immediately after a similar list for bishops and thus suggests a close relationship between the two offices. Second, it reinforces the scriptural evidence of Romans 16:1 that women are suitable to become deacons, for the writer gives two parallel and similar lists of qualifications, one for men deacons and one for "women." Third, the passage offers clues for selection based on public respect, and for family life based on elemental decency. Deacons, men and women, must be serious, discreet, temperate, and faithful. Like all Christians, deacons "must hold fast to the mystery of the faith with a clear conscience" (1 Tim. 3:9). Furthermore, they should be tested to see if they are "blameless," which may refer to a private assessment of character or even to a public examination before election or ratification. Male deacons should be "married only once" (whether concurrently or consecutively, the author does not say) and good managers of their families; presumably a similar standard applies to women. There is no mention of formation or function. Deacons who serve well "gain a good standing for themselves and great boldness in the faith that is in Christ Jesus." This promise does not refer to advancement to the presbyterate or episcopate, because sequential grades of Christian office are not mentioned in Scripture and remain foreign to church life for at least three more centuries.

Although actual deacons of the church are minor figures in the New Testament, the ancient tradition and theology whereby the Christian community orders itself constitutes a major element in God's scheme of creation. In our time the biblical tradition provides a guide to *diakonia* and deacons in the modern church. We need to keep in mind the scriptural sources. Against servitude to despotic masters stands service to a just and benevolent God. God's deliverance of the Hebrews out of oppression and slavery in Egypt moves them to render mercy and justice and to offer true worship. God's deliverance of all people from sin and death, through the servant of the Lord, Christ on the cross, encourages them to wash each other's feet and to break the bread of life.

13

✳

## CHAPTER TWO

# THE EARLY CHURCH

In the first three centuries the church adopted two practices that have inspired the modern revival of deacons. First, while continuing the ancient tradition of mercy and justice as an obligation of all the faithful, the church added the practice, in many places, of making deacons responsible for the institutional administration of charity. Second, the church began to use deacons as officers of the church, closely attached to the bishop, ordained as his helpers and co-workers. In the major evolutions of church life in the fourth and later centuries, however, both practices gradually underwent drastic changes, as the diaconate declined in importance, lost purpose, and eventually became absorbed, with other ministries, by the presbyterate. This concentration of many ministries in one order still affects the life, ministry, and liturgy of Christian communities. Our contemporary understanding of the diaconate—and of ministry in general—in the modern church thus rests partly on issues and problems raised in the early church.

## CHARITY AND LOVE

When modern Christians think of service, in the sense of charity, they often have in mind the church of the first three centuries, especially the first century, when believers "would sell their possessions and goods and distribute the proceeds to all, as any had need" (Acts 2:45). In many ways this ideal picture of life as a common and sacred bond was real. Early Christians practiced social charity as individuals and as a community; they collected funds for the poor, and the deacons administered practical care. In the local church of each city or central town, small, persecuted groups of believers lived close to each other and to the neighboring poor. They collected money for the needy at the Eucharist and communal meals, visited the sick and those in prison, and sent offerings to Jerusalem and the other churches.

The writings of the early church fathers strongly emphasize the element of *agape* in Christian life. One of the earliest non-canonical documents of the young church is the *Didache*, or *Teaching of the Twelve Apostles*, a Syrian text from early in the second century (c. 110). It begins with a statement about two ways, life and death. The way of life is the way of the great commandment: love God and love your neighbor. The way of life is closely associated with forgiveness, kindness, abstinence, and generosity. It is the way of love. About the year 95 Clement of Rome writes: "In love the Master took hold of us. For the sake of the love he had for us, Jesus Christ our Lord, by the will of God, gave his blood for us, his flesh for our flesh, and his life for our lives."[1]

The principal purpose of *agape*, as early Christians understood it, is to help the poor and others in need. This duty fell equally on all believers. In the middle of the second century Justin Martyr in his *First Apology* writes that the Christians in Rome share their wealth and property with needy persons. After the Eucharist, Justin says, the president distributes the collection to orphans and widows, the sick, prisoners, sojourners, and all in need. Tertullian in his *Apology* about the year 197 reports that Christians collect modest amounts of money and expend it

> for the burial of the poor, for boys and girls without parents and destitute, for the aged quietly confined to their homes, for the shipwrecked; and if there are any in the mines or in the islands or in the prisons, if it be for the reason that they are worshipers of God, then they become the foster sons of their confession. But it is mainly the practice of such a love which leads some to put a brand upon us. "See," they say, "how they love one another," for they themselves hate each other. "And how ready they are to die for one another," they themselves being more inclined to kill each other.

In the early church the *Didache*'s "way of life" was expressed also through a communal meal called an *agape*, or love feast. Practically speaking, the meal was a means of collecting money and food for social relief. Presided over by the bishop, or, if he were absent, by a presbyter or a deacon, the meal included prayers, readings, hymn singing, and the giving of pieces of blessed bread (not from the Eucharist). The *agape* meal incorporated elements of friendship and community, much like a parish covered-dish supper in the modern church, but its main purpose was charity. Under the supervision of a presbyter or a deacon, offerings and leftover food were distributed to the sick, widows, and poor.

Christians also continued the Jewish tradition of individual almsgiving and other relief, and the rich and privileged were expected to care for the poor and deprived. But social care was too essential a duty to leave to spontaneous charity or random philanthropy. The church had a strong perception of its corporate responsibility for care, and in each local church the chief agents for charity were deacons acting in the service of the bishop.

After the peace of Constantine in 313, however, the church gradually shifted from a small and familiar organism to a large and often remote institution. Although Christians in many places continued to practice *agape*, the church's picture of itself as a loving people became hazy. As an imperial institution, with a bureaucracy, terminology, and practices modeled on those of Rome, it absorbed itself in broad issues of doctrine and structure. Eventually, by the middle ages, the official exercise of charity became the obligation chiefly of parish priests and monastic communities. The role of deacons in the church eventually changed to reflect this shift in emphasis.[2]

## ORDAINED TO THE BISHOP

In the thirty years between Paul of Tarsus and Clement of Rome, the diaconate became established firmly in the young churches; in the second through the fourth centuries, it accumulated functions and symbols that have endured to the twentieth. When *diakonoi* were interpreted as the principal symbols of Jesus in the church, deacons began to acquire theological significance.

Three writers near the end of the first century mention deacons. The *Didache* instructs each local church: "Elect for yourselves, therefore, bishops and deacons worthy of the Lord, humble and not lovers of money, truthful and proven; for they also serve you in the ministry of the prophets and teachers." The deacons' assistance to their bishops presumably includes service at the eucharistic table. Clement of Rome introduces the typology, later widely copied, of the bishop and presbyter as the Hebrew priest, while the deacon is the Christian equivalent of the Hebrew Levite—a ritual waiter in a divinely ordered cult. *The Shepherd of Hermas*, dated early in the second century, depicts the church as a tower under construction in which the square, white fitting-stones are apostles, bishops, teachers, and deacons. Centuries later this metaphor reappears in some icons of deacons, who hold a church building in the left hand (and usually a censer in the right hand). *The Shepherd of Hermas* also rebukes deacons who plunder widows and orphans and otherwise profit from charity. These early documents tell us that deacons were elected as important officers in the church, acting in a community structure that included oversight of relief for the poor and needy.

Ignatius of Antioch, on his journey to martyrdom in Rome, wrote letters to seven churches. These letters mention deacons frequently; they are his "fellow servants," integral and respected officers in the church and personal assistants to the bishop. Ignatius is the first Christian to propose a symbolic structure for the three orders: "In like manner let everyone respect the deacons as they would respect Jesus Christ, and just as they respect the bishop as a type of the Father, and the presbyters as the council of God and college of apostles." As sacred symbols, derived from the relationship of Jesus with his Father, deacons are intimately connected with their bishop. They exercise important functions in liturgy and charity. In their active role within the sacred ministry of bishop, presbyters, and deacons, they are "dispensers of the mysteries of Jesus Christ" (a variant of the "mystery of the faith" in 1 Timothy). Yet they are not deacons of food and drink but officers of the church of God."[3] The two deacons who accompanied Ignatius on his journey carried his letters and the story of his martyrdom to the seven churches.

Still another writer of the second century who comments on deacons is Justin Martyr, whose *First Apology* gives us the first clear description of the liturgical duties of a deacon:

> After the president has given thanks and all the people
> have shouted their assent, those whom we call deacons
> give to each one present to partake of the eucharistic bread

and wine and water; and to those who are absent they
carry away a portion.

Justin doesn't mention other liturgical functions. Apparently at
this time the gospel was sung by a reader, but we do not know who
led the intercessions. It is worth noting that deacons administered
*both* the bread and the wine (according to ancient custom, mixed
with water for sobriety). In a letter supposedly written by Clement
of Rome, deacons are to be "as eyes to the bishop" by finding out
who is about to sin. Deacons are also to keep order in Christian
meetings and inform "the multitude" about the sick, so that they
may visit them and supply their needs under the bishop's direction.

We can tell a great deal about the meaning and functions of deacons in the early church from the *Apostolic Tradition*, attributed to
Hippolytus, a presbyter of Rome, about the year 215. This work, of
immense influence in modern revisions of liturgy, not only reveals
the prevailing customs in Rome at the start of the third century,
but also gives an indication of church order throughout the whole
ancient church over an extended period of time. Like a bishop or
presbyter, a deacon is elected by all the people of the local church
and ordained on the Lord's Day. At the ordination all give assent,
and the bishop lays hands on the person chosen, in silence, while
all pray for the descent of the Spirit. The author comments:

19

❊

> In ordaining a deacon, the bishop alone lays hands,
> because [a deacon] is ordained not to the priesthood but
> to the servanthood of the bishop, to carry out commands.
> [A deacon] does not take part in the council of the clergy,
> but attends to duties and makes known to the bishop what
> is necessary . . . .

After the silence, the bishop prays:

> God, who created all things and set them in order by the
> Word, Father of our Lord Jesus Christ, whom you sent to
> serve your will and to show us your desires, give the Holy
> Spirit of grace and care and diligence to this your servant,
> whom you have chosen to serve your church and to offer
> [to bring forward] in your holy of holies the gifts which
> are offered you by your appointed high priests, so that

serving without blame and with a pure heart, he may be
counted worthy of this high office and glorify you through
your Servant Jesus Christ.[4]

These accounts of ordination rites in ancient Rome have several
implications for the church in our time:

Selection. God chooses, as the ordination prayer says, but the
choice is wielded by the people of God. The *laos* elect a deacon. We
do not know exactly how the process of selection took place, but
apparently it involved a gathering of all the Christian people in a
city, the local church, who in some way chose one of their number.
The bishop's role in the process was to ordain on the next convenient Sunday—implying that he could also refuse to ordain.
Selection was thus swift and concentrated in the local assembly of
Christians, whereas in most churches today selection is lengthy
and spread among several select committees.

Terminology. In the early house churches "priesthood" referred
primarily to Christ. Later it became the term for bishops, and
finally for bishops and presbyters. In this development "priesthood" and "clergy" included the bishop (the high priest) and his
presbyters, but not his deacons. Although deacons did not belong
to the clergy, they were also not members of a separate group called
laity. At that time *laos* still meant all the people of God. The distinction between clergy (*kleros*, or those on the rolls) and laity (*laos*,
or people) was only beginning to be worked out. (By the end of the
third century, deacons and maybe others were considered members
of a distinct body called clergy.) Like all Christians, deacons were
members of the *laos*, ordained to *diakonia* but not to the priestly
college called *kleros*. This early practice stands in contrast to the
later, and still current, treatment of clergy and laity as two separate
bodies within the one church.

Relationships. Ordination rites symbolize ministerial relationships on several different primary levels. In ancient Rome, the *laos*
elected bishops, presbyters, and deacons; hence all three orders had
a fundamental relationship with the baptized body of Christ, from
whose ranks the ordinand came. This ancient practice has important implications today for connections among church leaders.
Within the orders of both bishops and presbyters there is strong
collegiality as the "priesthood" (of the bishop). The ministerial
relationship of deacons, the diaconal college, is primarily with the

20
✳

bishop and not with each other or with the presbyters. The role of deacons as members of the bishop's household or staff, however, provides them with collegial harmony as the "servanthood of the bishop." A healthy community of deacons means healthy deacons.

Theology. The opening phrases of the ordination prayer set forth a theology of the diaconate based on Christ as eternal Word and incarnate Servant. God "created all things and set them in order by the Word," and God the Father sent Christ "to serve your will and to show us your desires." Word and Servant are thus scriptural types of the church and the deacon. God's ordering of creation is a type of God's ordering of the church, and the service of Christ (who reveals God and carries out the work of ordered creation) is a type of the service of the deacon. Deacon is to bishop as Word is to God, servant Christ to Father. Like Ignatius of Antioch, therefore, the author of *Apostolic Tradition* provides a basis for the symbolic appreciation of deacons today.

Functions. The ordination prayer also reveals two areas of function. First, the deacon ordained to the servanthood (or service or ministry, probably *diakonia* in the lost Greek original) of the bishop is "to serve" the church. The term probably refers not primarily to care of the poor and needy but rather to ecclesial roles such as speaking for, acting for, and attending on the bishop in several important areas. These areas included social care but were not limited to them. Second, the deacon is "to offer"—or, preferably, to bring forward—in the Eucharist the gifts offered by the high priest (bishop). These are two different but related liturgical offerings. The deacon presents the people's offerings of bread and wine mixed with water to the bishop, and the bishop offers them to God in the eucharistic prayer. Thus we have the ancient foundation for an ordained ministry that must function both in the world and in the church, as focused in the actions and ministerial relationships of the liturgy.

Another third-century document, the *Didascalia Apostolorum* (Teaching of the Apostles), paints a rich picture of the evolving office of deacon, both male and female.[5] Here the deacon's work for the bishop clearly included social welfare: visiting all in need and informing the bishop about those in distress, accepting alms for the bishop, helping the bishop supervise the order of widows. In this *diakonia* of *agape* (ministry of love) the deacon worked closely with the bishop, "a single soul dwelling in two bodies," often as a full-time, paid factotum, and this activity carried over into the liturgy. One deacon stood by the oblations, and another guarded the door as the people entered. The deacon inside saw that each person went to the proper place (in a congregation segregated by ecclesiastical status, sex, and age) and prevented whispering, sleeping, laughter, and signaling. The deacon made announcements and at the kiss of peace called out, "Is there anyone who holds a grudge against his companion?" In baptism the bishop alone invoked the name of God, but both bishop and deacons were involved with undressing, oiling, completing the oiling, dressing, and giving ethical instruction. In Gaza women deacons stayed for eight days with newly baptized young women who were orphans. In short, deacons did whatever needed to be done.[6]

The deacon described in early church orders and by the author of *Apostolic Tradition* and many others comes alive in the person of Laurence of Rome. The church of Rome limited its deacons to seven, based on the precedent of Acts 6, and each administered a diaconal district, one of the seven hills of Rome. As the *diaconus episcopi*, or bishop's deacon, with especially close and personal ties to his bishop, Laurence had custody of alms for the poor. On 7 August 258, bishop Sixtus II and his seven deacons were arrested in the Roman catacombs. As Sixtus and the six other deacons were being carried away for beheading, Laurence cried after him, "Regarding him to whom you entrusted the consecration of the Savior's blood, to whom you have granted fellowship in partaking of the sacraments, would you refuse him a sharing in your death?"[7] (In less stilted English this is perhaps better translated: "Holy priest, don't leave me! We shared the blood of Christ. Let's share each other's blood.") Laurence was kept alive because he knew where the silver and gold were. Finally he gathered the poor, the lame, and the blind for whom he had cared, showed them to the city prefect, and said, "These are the treasures of the church." He was martyred on August 10, supposedly roasted alive on a gridiron but probably beheaded like his bishop.

Another early deacon with close ties to his bishop was Vincent of Saragossa, martyred on 22 January 304. Vincent was not only the eyes and ears of his bishop, but literally his mouth. Because Valerius stuttered badly, Vincent often preached for him. According to legend, they were arrested by the governor of Spain, threatened with torture and death, and pressured to renounce their faith. Vincent said, "Father, if you order me, I will speak." Valerius replied, "Son, as I have committed you to dispense the word of God, so I now charge you to answer in vindication of the faith which we defend." Vincent defied the governor and was tortured to death.

As with the men, the legends of women deacon saints of the early church tell us more than any other document. In addition to Phoebe, these saints include a prominent martyr, the aged Apollonia, burned to death by a mob in Alexandria on 2 February 249. Refusing to renounce the faith, she walked into a bonfire her tormentors had set. Because they first knocked out her teeth, she became the patron of dentists and toothache victims. According to an apocryphal legend in the early church, the female martyr Thekla was converted in the 50s or 60s at Iconium, became a deacon (perhaps), and after much persecution for her dedication to virginity, was martyred at the age of ninety. Thekla was immensely popular in the early church. The Orthodox honor her as the first woman martyr, parallel to Stephen, with a feast day on September 23.

Scholars may question the historical accuracy of these legends about Laurence and Vincent, Apollonia and Thekla, and other early martyrs, but their stories tell us a good deal about deacons in the early church. They stood close to their bishop, they brought help to the poor and brought the word to the people, and they held the mystery of the faith with a clear conscience, even to death.

The end of the third century and beginning of the fourth was a time of great change for the church and its deacons. After Constantine and his co-emperor adopted a policy of toleration for the Christian church in 313, which thus began to grow, new rules evolved to define the roles of deacons. Some of these governed the moral and sexual conduct of presbyters and deacons. In about 250 Cyprian and other bishops had written with approval of the excommunication of a deacon "who dallied often with a virgin," while later on there may also have been concern about nepotism. At the end of the third century, the reform-minded Council of Elvira tried to impose celibacy with the rule, widely ignored, that bishops, presbyters, and deacons "are to keep themselves away from their wives and are not to beget children," while the Council of Ancyra in 314 set the rule that deacons may marry after ordination only if they announce their intention to marry before ordination; otherwise they are to be deposed. The early purpose of celibacy was to prevent church property from getting into private hands.

Rules governing clerical conduct were repeated and reinforced by the Council of Nicaea in 325. No cleric may have a woman living with him, except his mother, sister, aunt, or other woman beyond suspicion (Canon 4). Because of "great disorder and contentions," no cleric is allowed "to move from city to city" (Canon 15). Specifically about deacons, Canon 18 reveals a drift in practice and is ominous for future discipline: Deacons must keep within their rank, not sit with the presbyters, and not give communion to presbyters, for they are "the servants of the bishop and . . . less than presbyters." By the end of the fourth century, a male deacon is defined in negative terms. He may not bless, baptize, or offer the Eucharist, although he may excommunicate those of lesser rank. A subdeacon, lector, cantor, and deaconess may do even less, "for they are the inferior of deacons."[8] The church of this period seemed more interested in hierarchical rank than in service of the bishop defined as ministry carrying out the work of God.

The most celebrated eastern deacon of this period was Ephrem, whom the Syrians called "the harp of the Holy Spirit." He may have accompanied his bishop, James of Nisibis, to the Council of Nicaea. After the fall of Nisibis to the Persians in 363, he retired to a cave near Edessa, where he lived a harsh life, preached in the city, cared for the poor and sick, and wrote hymns, sung by a choir of women, as a weapon against the Gnostic and Arian heresies. In combating heresy, Ephrem considered himself an agent of his bishop. His writings in Syriac are famous both for their scriptural inspiration and metaphorical style. Still another Syrian poet was the deacon Romanos the Melodist, who in the sixth century moved to Constantinople, where he wrote metrical sermons and hymns. Some of his *kontakia*, brief hymns in the form of prayer, are still sung in eastern churches.

Several women deacons are remembered partly because of famous relatives or friends, such as Nonna, mother of the bishop Gregory Nazianzus. In another prominent family of the fourth century, the bishops Gregory of Nyssa and Basil the Great had as their elder sister the deacon Macrina the Younger, famous in her own right as head of a community of nuns on the family estate in Cappadocia; her friend the deacon Lampadia led a chorus of virgins. In Constantinople the deacon Olympias, a rich widow, ran a convent called the Olympiados that included four deacons and some two hundred fifty virgins. She taught catechumens and cared for widows, the old, the sick, and the poor. When John Chrysostom, the new bishop, arrived in 397, she became his friend, advisor, and benefactor, and upon his exile she suffered persecution from his enemies.

The church of the West apparently had few women deacons, and they were mainly in Gaul. The most famous Gallican deacon is Radegund of Poitiers, who died in 587. As a child she was kidnapped from Thuringia and eventually forced to marry the brutish king Clothaire I of the Franks. She endured him for ten years until he murdered her brother. Radegund then fled to Noyon, where she persuaded the bishop to ordain her a deacon, and began a ministry of caring for the sick, including lepers, and visiting prisoners. After her ordination she founded Holy Cross monastery near Poitiers, which at her death numbered some two hundred nuns. Her friend the poet Venantius Honorius Fortunatus wrote hymns in honor of the sliver of the true Cross housed in her monastery, *Vexilla Regis prodeunt* and *Pange lingua* (*The Hymnal 1982*, Hymns 161, 162, 165, and 166).

Deacons did not vanish after the fourth century, and no "Golden Age" (as some have dubbed the first three centuries) gave way to a "Leaden Age." Every age is both golden and leaden. Few scholars, however, have traced the steps of deacons over that great expanse of history, the middle ages and early modern age. The reality is that deacons remained visible and active in the lives of many parish churches and cathedrals, in big cities and small villages. As Christian life increasingly focused on the Mass and on those who celebrated that holy sacrifice, originally called presbyters and later priests, the diaconate shrank in both permanence and substance. The practice of sequential ordination—ordaining persons to a prior order in preparation for a later order—originated in the early church as a means of gaining experience in ordained ministry. In a common pattern during the first millennium, persons were ordained as deacons at age twenty-five before ordination as presbyters five years later. The practice was not universal, however, and in Rome for several centuries none of the powerful seven (later fourteen) deacons became presbyters, which would have been a step down. Instead, several of them rose to the papacy without passing through the presbyterate. In the twelfth century sequential ordination became a canonical obligation in the West, and it also put on a theological cloak: the diaconate was regarded as necessary for priestly character, and hence as indelible. Once a deacon, always a deacon, as some still say, but deacons as priests, not as deacons.[9]

## THE LESSONS OF THE EARLY DIACONATE

The development of the diaconate in the first three centuries and the changes over subsequent centuries are not isolated incidents in the history of the early church. They have meaning today, shedding light on issues in the modern church and providing guidance for our understanding.

One of these is the question of women deacons. The Episcopal Church and most other provinces of the Anglican Communion ordain women as deacons. The Roman Catholic Church resists ordaining them, citing a tradition of masculinity in the order, and the Orthodox, despite their tradition of women deacons, even in recent times, are hesitant. Even in places where women deacons are accepted, they are sometimes treated as inferior to men deacons. The historical evidence, however, supports the ordination of women as deacons. In the early church women deacons functioned in ways parallel to the role of men deacons, caring for women and children as men cared for men, although they often had subordinate status. Numerous and widespread in the East, especially in Syria and Greece, women deacons flourished in the fourth through the seventh centuries and continued to function in Constantinople until the twelfth century. Although less numerous in the West, they were ordained in Gaul and other areas where women exercised authority. There may even have been a few in Rome, where Jerome corresponded with a woman deacon but never admitted the existence of women deacons. The ordination rites for women paralleled those for men, and they received the *orarion*, or stole. Frequently these women were the wives of men deacons or presbyters, until mandatory celibacy abolished clerical families. Some were the wives of bishops; when the man was made a bishop and separated from his wife, the woman, if suited for the office, became a deacon. Some were abbesses, who by custom had to be deacons.

In the East, men and women deacons functioned both pastorally and liturgically. In the Eucharist women deacons ministered together in church, oversaw and made announcements to the women, who were seated off to one side or in the gallery, led their responses, supervised their offerings, and administered their communion. They arranged the lamps, washed the vessels, and mixed the water and wine in the chalice. In liturgies composed only of women, they read the lessons and taught. In baptism, in which the candidates were nude, they anointed and clothed the female neophytes. They took communion to the housebound and chaperoned interviews between male clerics and women. The *Didascalia*, expanding on Ignatius of Antioch, says that the woman deacon stands "in the position of the Holy Spirit."

In the West, after about the fourth century, the position of women deacons appears to have suffered as a result of the high regard in which virgins were held, a regard not extended to widows. When women deacons reached Gaul, typically it was widows who became deacons. Most likely their duties were similar to those in the East, with an emphasis on teaching. The document of Nicaea has something to tell us about the status of women deacons. In mentioning the problem of the Paulianists, anti-Trinitarian heretics who are returning to the church, Canon 19 of Nicaea states that they are to be rebaptized, and their clergy reordained or deposed. "However, we note concerning those who have assumed the garb of deaconess: because they have not had any ordination, they are to be numbered among the laity."[10] The feminine form *diakonissa* appears here for the first time in a legal document. By referring to the garbed but unordained heretics as lay persons, the canon implies that ordained women deacons (who also wear special dress) are members of the clergy.

After the fourth century, presbyters became parish priests, and bishops became the administrators of large dioceses. With this change, only a few highly placed deacons could be the eyes and ears of the bishop, and most deacons became instead clerics in transit to the priesthood. Before, deacons were the agents of the bishop's oversight of *agape* in the parish; after, they tended to be actors playing a liturgical bit part. This shift resulted in a new distinction between diocesan and parish deacons, one that has reappeared in our time. Before the fourth century, deacons in a church or parish had been a small group attached to the bishop, like Laurence of Rome, who is a classic example of the early diaconate. After the peace of Constantine, however, deacons became scattered throughout the diocese and served as pastoral assistants to presbyters. Eventually they became detached from their bishop, were seen as inferior to presbyters, and functioned mainly in the liturgy—

27

servants not so much of *agape* in the fullest sense as of sacred rites alone, on the threshold of the priesthood.

We have a similar situation in the modern church. Because bishops are chief pastors of dioceses, not pastors of parishes, requiring deacons to serve directly under the bishop means something vastly different from what it meant to Laurence or Vincent. Parish pastors in most denominations function much as early bishops did—except that they may not ordain. The question for the modern church is twofold: first, how is the deacon to serve adequately under both bishop and priest, and second, how is the bishop to get back in the business of overseeing *agape*?

Another issue facing the contemporary church is the balance of roles in the liturgy according to order and appropriate function. In the second century, the scriptural definition of *diakonos* as chief factotum was fully acted out in the Eucharist—deacons set the table and served the bread and wine. In the third century, deacons invited the people to exchange the kiss of peace, received the offerings of bread and wine, and brought them to the bishop, but they served only the wine. By the fourth century, diaconal functions expanded into the liturgy of the word. Deacons began to represent angels and messengers as well as table waiters. They proclaimed the gospel (formerly read by a reader), sang litanies of intercession, announced stages of the liturgy, and at the paschal vigil blessed the candle.

Gradually, however, priests took over the diaconal functions. This assumption resulted in a loss to both orders, and hence in a loss of symbolism for the church. As the priesthood reached to include within itself all ministries, it lost focus and priestly presence. The main priestly function, singing the eucharistic prayer, became reduced to a mostly inaudible mumble in an action barely visible to the congregation. As the diaconate became absorbed into the priesthood, as a step on the hierarchical pyramid, it too lost presence, the special significance of those who are publicly visible as agents of the church and who spend their lives in active service. The roles of priest and deacon became unbalanced.

In modern liturgies throughout the West, the church has recovered almost everything deacons slowly accumulated over the first four centuries. The issue facing the church now is keeping a balance among a diversity of many roles. Deacons may share some of their role with other members of the *laos;* the Episcopal Church does not restrict the prayers of the people or the administration of the sacrament to deacons. Some other Anglican churches, following the practice in the first three centuries, will even allow any baptized person to proclaim the gospel. Bishops and presbyters may relinquish to others some of their (usually minor) functions in the liturgy, but the other members of the *laos* also need to show restraint by respecting the liturgical tradition of the early church. Liturgy should accurately symbolize both the priesthood of Christ and the *diakonia* carried out on the cross and in the world.

The issue of diversity of roles, however, deals with far more than orderly worship. Liturgy reflects the entire life of the church, and the balance of roles in the liturgical assembly reveals all too accurately how the bishop, presbyters, deacons, and all the faithful of a diocese relate to each other, minister in the church and the world, and serve the will of God.

✳

# EPISCOPAL CHURCH:
# EARLY DEACONS

Until recent decades, the deacon most churchgoers saw and knew was a young man in an interim state. After graduating from seminary, he awaited his ordination to the priesthood, passed a brief internship, and learned his craft from an older, wiser priest. This temporary office inherited from the classic diaconate only the name and liturgy of deacon. By its nature it was intended neither to provide *diakonia* to the poor and needy, nor to assist the bishop in important matters, but to season apprentice clerics in sacerdotal and—particularly after the Reformation—pastoral ministry. This view of the diaconate was common to the Anglican, Roman Catholic, Orthodox, and some protestant churches. But early in the nineteenth century, renewal movements, evangelical and catholic revivals, the rediscovery of patristic sources, new attitudes toward the poor, and new opportunities in mission fields slowly caused the churches to respond with experiments in diaconal ministry.

Since the early nineteenth century, the Episcopal Church in particular has seen four types, or "waves," of deacons: missionary or indigenous deacons (male), deaconesses (female), perpetual deacons (male), and deacons today (male and female).[1] These categories are not neatly exclusive; to a large extent they overlap. But they demonstrate that the order of deacons has developed and changed as the church has responded to the needs of the world in different historical circumstances. In this chapter I will speak of the first three waves, the early deacons who preceded the deacons of today.

31

✳

## MISSIONARY OR INDIGENOUS DEACONS

The missionary or indigenous deacon, existing from the 1840s through the 1930s and usually ordained on an ad hoc basis, was virtually unknown to most Episcopalians in settled parts of the nation, and was rare even on the frontier. His ministry was diverse and often eccentric, as the following stories will reveal. The first deacon in the Episcopal Church of whom we have extensive knowledge worked in what is now the diocese of Western North Carolina. In 1842 Bishop Levi S. Ives of North Carolina decided to begin mission work in a wild area near Boone where two valleys cross. He bought two thousand acres and called the area Valle Crucis. There Ives established a monastic community called the Society of the Holy Cross, and for the first monk he professed a farmer, William West Skiles.

Skiles was born in North Dakota and came to Valle Crucis in 1844 at the age of thirty-seven. He supervised the farming operation and dairy herd, taught school, kept store, practiced medicine, raised funds to build the local Church of St. John the Baptist (contributing a third of the $700 construction cost), and became the spiritual leader of the community. Bishop Ives ordained Skiles a deacon in August 1847. In 1852 Ives resigned his office, sold the land, and became a Roman Catholic. The monastic order and school disbanded, but Skiles was the only one of the original monks not to marry. "Brother Skiles," as he was called, continued to care for the poor valley people until he died on 8 December 1862, and his body was buried next to the church he helped to build.[2]

Skiles was a missionary deacon, ordained to provide for religious life on the frontier. As the American people pushed west, beyond the settled life of the eastern seaboard, the need grew for trained missionaries who were part of frontier society. There were probably priests and deacons ordained casually to fill the needs of remote communities. Rather late, in 1871, by a resolution of General Convention, the church finally made canonical provision for these deacons. From 1871 through 1904, under this canon, men were ordained as deacons for missionary fields and ethnic—especially Native American—communities to which they were indigenous.

Two outstanding examples of missionary or indigenous deacons ordained in the late nineteenth century are Milnor Jones and David Pendleton Oakerhater. In 1895 Bishop Joseph Blount Cheshire of

North Carolina decided to revive the Valle Crucis mission around another fascinating character. This was Milnor Jones, born in 1848 of a prominent Maryland family, who fought as a Confederate soldier and then became a lawyer in Texas before suffering injury in a riding accident. Left with a limp, he devoted the rest of his life to God. After graduating from seminary at Sewanee and being ordained deacon in 1876, he decided to remain a deacon and, in the words of his bishop, to make himself "all things to the lowly whom he had chosen for his own." Most of his work was among the poor people of Western North Carolina, in 1879–92 around Tryon and in 1894–96 at Valle Crucis. He died in Baltimore in 1916.

We know about Jones from his biographer, Bishop Cheshire. *Milnor Jones, Deacon and Missionary* (actually a long obituary, dated 1916) was published in the diocesan newspaper and later as a pamphlet. Jones was outspoken, crusty, and cantankerous, qualities that delighted the bishop. He was especially fond of denouncing the local Baptists and Methodists, and sometimes came close to inciting a riot. One mob of unruly men even threatened the bishop. Nevertheless, Bishop Cheshire took delight in a deacon "who did not scruple on occasion to tell his bishop that the sermon he [the bishop] had just preached, 'did no more good than pouring water on a duck's back.'" An undisciplined oddball who cared nothing for settled work, and who preferred to minister in backwoods places, Jones traveled the mountain trails in the saddle, made friends of all he met, handed out prayer books, baptized everyone he could (often by immersion in a nearby creek), preached wild sermons from house to house, and only on rare occasion encountered his bishop, a priest, or any other member of the Episcopal establishment.

Another early deacon was David Pendleton Oakerhater of Oklahoma, whose Cheyenne name means "Sundancer" or "Making Medicine." Oakerhater was a war chief; as a young man, he distinguished himself for bravery as a member of an elite Cheyenne warrior society. After the futile battle of Adobe Walls in 1874, in which warriors of five tribes attacked a camp of white buffalo hunters in Texas, he was captured as one of the ringleaders and taken in chains, without trial, to the cavalry post at Fort Sill, Oklahoma. Later he was moved to Fort Marion, an old military prison at St. Augustine, Florida. In prison Oakerhater showed his natural leadership and was placed in charge of Indian youth there. He also drew sketches of Cheyenne life, using colored pencils and paper, and gave archery and art lessons to visitors. Mainly through his friendship with the young daughter of Senator George Hunt Pendleton of Ohio, he converted to Christianity, was sent to upstate New York to receive a Christian education, and was baptized on 6 October 1878.

Ordained deacon on 7 June 1881, Oakerhater left immediately for the Cheyenne nation of Oklahoma accompanied by a white priest, John B. Wicks. He returned to the people he had once led in war. When he met their leaders for the first time as a Christian he spoke in words long remembered among the Cheyenne. His address began:

> Men, you all know me. You remember when I led you
> out to war I went first and what I told you was true.
> Now I have been away to the east and I have learned
> about another captain, the Lord Jesus Christ, and he is
> my leader. He goes first, and all he tells me is true. I
> come back to my people to tell you to go with me now
> in this new road, a war that makes all for peace, and
> where we [ever] have only victory.[3]

34

In the Indian territory of northwest Oklahoma, Oakerhater touched the lives of hundreds of Cheyenne through his counseling, preaching, baptizing, and teaching. Within three years the whole Cheyenne nation converted to Christ. Among the new Christians was Whirlwind, a great peace chief, who at the turn of the century gave land for the new Episcopal mission at an old Indian village near Watonga. This religious and educational center for the Cheyenne still bears the name of Whirlwind Mission of the Holy Family. In 1904 Oakerhater opened a school at the mission that lasted until 1917, when the church closed it under government pressure.

The priest left after three years because of ill health, and soon Oakerhater was alone. The leaders of the Episcopal Church abandoned work among the Indians in Oklahoma. For twelve years Oakerhater was the only ordained Episcopalian in what is now the state of Oklahoma. Even after he retired in 1917 on a small pension, he continued to counsel and preach, marry the young and bury the dead, baptize, visit the sick, and find food for the hungry, until he died in 1931.

Many other Native Americans ministered as deacons among their people. By the 1860s, Dakota deacons included Daniel C. Hemans, Philip Johnson Wahpehan (called Philip the Deacon), and Christian Taopi (a former warrior, called Wounded One). The Kiowa deacon Paul Zotom traveled with Oakerhater on his trip west in 1881, but his work soon failed. Thomas P. Ashley ministered among the Sioux around the turn of the century until he was divorced in 1907. A Canadian of mixed Indian and white ancestry, Wellington Jefferson Salt worked with the Chippewa from 1911 until his death in 1920. Athabascan deacons include William Loola of Fort Yukon, Alaska, ordained in 1903, and Albert Tritt, ordained in the 1920s.[4]

These missionary or indigenous deacons of the nineteenth and early twentieth centuries functioned more as priests than as deacons. Often solitary, exercising their ministries without oversight and rarely in contact with their bishop, these men kept the Christian faith alive among their people. They presided over a community and built it up by preaching, teaching, and caring. These deacons administered the sacraments in every way except the one essential to leading a community in the complete Christian life: they were not permitted to preside at the Eucharist.

## DEACONESSES

The deaconess movement arose out of a sincere desire in many churches to organize women to work with the poor and sick. In the early nineteenth century this desire emerged in the Lutheran churches of Germany and helped shape a definition of *diakonia* that has lasted until the present: care of the needy. In the middle ages, social care was handled mainly by parish priests and monastic orders, but by the sixteenth century this system of charity had begun to break down. In the early nineteenth century, in the rubble of the Napoleonic wars and the human wreckage of the industrial age, secular and Christian social reformers drew attention to the plight of the poor, and both the evangelical revival and the Oxford movement awakened interest in social care as a crucial concern of the church. In Germany in 1831 the Lutheran pastor Theodor Fliedner founded a training institution at Kaiserswerth for women deaconesses after the New Testament model. Their pastors "consecrated" them, although Lutherans did not consider this ordination. These women began with ministries such as visiting the sick and poor in the parish, teaching young children and girls, and bringing ill children back to their infirmary for nursing. They shaped the Kaiserswerth institution into the deaconess motherhouse (sisterhood or association) movement, exercising a ministry of social welfare that flourishes to this day. In 1849 Fliedner brought four Lutheran deaconesses to Pittsburgh, Pennsylvania, and began a work that continues in the twenty-first century. Florence Nightingale trained at Kaiserswerth in 1851 and returned to England to found a secular school for nurses.

Anglicans in England and America soon attempted to imitate Fliedner, and in England a group of women dedicated themselves in 1861 "to minister to the necessities of the church" as "servants of the church." On 18 July 1862 Bishop Archibald Campbell Tait of London (who had visited Kaiserswerth in 1855) admitted Elizabeth Ferard to the office of deaconess with the laying on of hands. Ferard was thus the first woman deacon in the Church of England after a lapse of several centuries. She founded a community of women in 1861 that gradually grew into a religious order of deaconesses still in existence, the (formerly Deaconess) Community of St. Andrew.[5]

In America interest in the German deaconess movement began earlier than in England but did not immediately result in ordained deaconesses. In 1845 William Augustus Muhlenberg, rector of the Church of the Holy Communion in New York City, formed a sisterhood based on the German model. The first formal admission of deaconesses in the Episcopal Church took place forty years later in Alabama. The first bishop of Alabama, Nicholas H. Cobbs, planned a cathedral in Montgomery with a group of institutions around the building and, more important, around the bishop as "the heart" of the diocese. These were to include a house for deacons (for missionary and pastoral work) and a house for deaconesses (for care of the sick and poor), but the Civil War interrupted these plans. In late December 1864 his successor, Richard Hooker Wilmer, "instituted"—without laying on hands—three deaconesses, who formed a sisterhood after the Kaiserswerth model, with a constitution and rules approved by the bishop, and set to work caring for the many orphans left by the war. By 1885

Wilmer had overcome his scruples about imposing hands, and he set apart two deaconesses, Mary W. Johnson on Epiphany and Mary Caroline Friggell on St. Peter's Day. Strictly speaking, they were the first ordained deaconesses in the Episcopal Church.[6]

In 1889 General Convention passed Canon 10, "Of Deaconesses," which remained in effect, occasionally amended, until it was repealed in 1970. The existence of the canon was the result of the lobbying efforts, starting in 1871, of William Reed Huntington, rector of Grace Church, New York City. His parish immediately provided facilities for deaconesses and established a training center called Huntington House. Other training schools were opened in San Francisco, New Orleans, Minneapolis, Philadelphia, Berkeley, and Chicago. Most of these, funded by the diocese or local supporters, encountered financial difficulties and soon closed. Some became general training schools. In 1953, with the help of Millard Street, bishop suffragan of Chicago, the Central House for Deaconesses was established in Evanston, Illinois. This continued in existence until it changed its name in 1974 to the National Center for the Diaconate.

Deaconesses in the Episcopal Church were "unmarried or widowed"—that is, celibate—for most of the existence of the order. A substantial change in the canon occurred in 1964, when General Convention, in response to the spirit of the times, removed the phrase "unmarried or widowed." But the ancient order, as restored in the Episcopal Church, had already begun to decline. Thus the final form of Canon 51, "Of Deaconesses," adopted in 1964, begins:

> A woman of devout character and proved fitness may be ordered Deaconess by any Bishop of this Church, subject to the provisions of this Canon.

The canon goes on to list charitable and pastoral functions. A deaconess is to care for "the sick, the afflicted, and the poor," to instruct in the faith, to prepare candidates for baptism and confirmation, to "work among women and children," and to "organize and carry on social work" (including the education of women and children). They are also to assist at baptism, to read the daily offices and litany "in the absence of the Minister," and when licensed by the bishop "to give instruction or deliver addresses at such services."

37

✳

Above all else, the order of deaconesses was a service order with a strong sense of community. Although its members often lived apart and in lonely circumstances, they supported each other in prayer, giving, and the common life. It was a society of women church workers, an historic order of deaconesses, and a quasi-religious order—a community of sisters with distinctive dress and pectoral cross, austere lifestyle, and concept of social work. Although the dress appeared to many to be a religious habit, it was modeled on Kaiserswerth apparel or common female dress of the early nineteenth century, with a simple veil and collar. In England celibacy was not required except in the Community of St. Andrew; there was a married deaconess as early as the 1880s. Deaconesses worked in many different settings: as parish assistants, teachers, institutional and school administrators, prison and hospital chaplains, inner-city workers, and missionaries, often in remote areas such as Appalachia and Nevada. A few were wealthy, but most lived in poverty and performed hard work for low wages over many years of loyal dedication.

One important source for the work of deaconesses is the dozen diaries and hundreds of letters, pictures, and other artifacts of Mary Douglass Burnham (1832–1904), which her great-granddaughter found in a trunk in the attic. Long before she was set apart as deaconess, Burnham helped to found the Dakota League in Massachusetts in 1864, in support of Indian missions, and in the 1870s she went to work among the Ponka tribe in Nebraska. There she taught women and girls to sew. Her letters indicate the practical nature of Christian charity which deaconesses had to perform. In one letter she writes, "Between women sitting on the floor, some with babies strapped to a board beside them or older ones crawling around, it requires considerable dexterity to get from one side to the other without doing any damage." She also assisted the sick and dying, although she knew "so little about sickness that I don't venture much beyond Nitro for fever and Quinine for chills." Throughout her life she remained keenly interested in Indian work and influenced Oakerhater in his conversion to Christianity. Later she served as head of several charity institutions and hospitals until shortly before her death.[7]

During World War II another deaconess, Julia A. Clark, spent five years in Yunan, China, in the war-torn district of Hankow. Her work included carrying supplies to hospital bases and helping with nursing. She was several times under bomb attack; often she had to prepare bodies for burial. Her story includes one account interesting for its implications about liturgy and authority:

> Perhaps some of you may be shocked when I tell you of another thing that I did. The clergy were hard-pressed. Near the air bases, there would sometimes be over 100 aviators at the Holy Communion. One of the missionary bishops over there asked me to assist, I being a deaconess. I could only ask him to speak to my bishop and to the other bishops. You see, the Church is all one Church in China—English, Chinese, American—all making one Holy Catholic Church. I told the Chinese bishop that I was the American deaconess, and that American deaconesses did not assist at the Holy Communion. And he said, "You are a Chinese deaconess out here." Everyone consented, so I thought it right to do what I was asked to do. I administered the cup. I thought that I would wear just a cotta, but they had me wear a surplice, and they insisted upon a stole. So I wore that also, over the shoulder as a deacon does.[8]

The order of deaconesses also included feisty characters. One was Mary Sandys Hutton, who worked in the Blue Ridge Mountains of Virginia from 1934 on. This remarkable woman was paralyzed from polio and had walked on crutches since the age of three. Nevertheless, she founded missions, directed a doctor's clinic and a clothing bureau, visited mountain homes, preached, conducted prayer book services, held revivals, ran a school bus, and sponsored children for baptism (as a deaconess, she was not allowed to baptize), many of whom were named after her. Several documents testify to the love and respect in which mountain folk held her. At her funeral the preacher recalled one incident. Hutton was conducting morning prayer at a remote mission where the people were not speaking to each other. She decided to delay the service until there was peace.

> "I want everybody here to turn to the person next to him and shake hands," she said. "If you can say, 'I'm glad you're

here,' do it. If you can't, don't. You won't fool God and you won't fool me. But you can shake hands."

"They just stared at me and did nothing," she remembered. "I said, 'I'm not going to start services until you do. You can have a Christian church or belong to the devil.' They shook hands."

On another occasion a mountaineer came into her house with a shotgun and announced that he had a message from God to kill her. "That's strange," she said. "I was just talking to God, and he didn't mention it to me. Perhaps we'd better talk to him together." After an hour or so the man departed, leaving his shotgun. The deaconess sent it back to him.[9]

Another spunky deaconess was Harriet Mary Bedell (1875–1969), who spent ten years at Whirlwind Mission in Oklahoma and sixteen years with Indians in Alaska before coming to the Mikasuki tribe of the Seminoles. In Florida she lived in a simple four-room house on the Tamiami Trail, in the midst of the Everglades. The Mikasuki gradually came to trust her, and she was the only white person they would speak to. In her old age the diocese wanted her to move into a religious community, but she said, "No. No. This is my place. They need me, and I am not frightened out here. The Indians are always watching me, just as God is watching over me." During more than a quarter-century with the Mikasuki, she converted some of the families, but the Seminoles as a tribe were not ready to accept Christ. In 1960 she quoted one old medicine man, "You just keep on telling us, and by'm by we do what you say."[10]

In Nevada the presence of indefatigable and underpaid deaconesses in many of the rural communities of the 1930s and 40s helped to pave the way for acceptance of new forms of women's ministry in the 1970s and 80s. At Pyramid Lake, on the Northern Band Paiute Reservation, older women remembered the presence of "the nuns" (deaconesses in habits) who worked as medical missionaries in conjunction with a circuit-riding physician, catechized the children and young people, and did a wide variety of other ministries.

One Nevada deaconess, Lydia Ramsay, worked at St. Andrews, Battle Mountain, in the late 1930s. Her ministry illustrates the gifts that women can bring to isolated communities in a harsh environment. One of her responsibilities was coordinating a program called Church School by Mail. She would drive the unpaved roads of northern Nevada's vast range land looking for children to enroll. Her preferred tactic was to do her scouting on wash day. Anytime she saw children's clothes on the wash line she would stop and visit, and sign the family up.

One of Nevada's historic deaconesses was active until the 1990s. Mary Hetler ministered at Christ Church, Pioche, as deaconess in charge, and she served the diocese as a whole through her work in Christian education and at the diocesan camp, Galilee. In the latter capacity she usually picked up and delivered children along her route from Pioche to Lake Tahoe—a trip of roughly 450 miles each way. Later she married Jim Bradshaw and moved to nearby Caliente; as was customary in those days, she was deposed from the diaconate upon her marriage. Her ministry, however, continued. Half a century after her setting apart, restored to the diaconate, Mary Bradshaw coordinated senior citizens' transportation for all of remote Lincoln County.[11]

Deaconesses worked among the mountaineers of Virginia, the range dwellers of Nevada, the Cheyenne of Oklahoma, the Ponkas of Nebraska, the Eskimos and Athabascans of Alaska, the Seminoles of Florida, the Lakota of South Dakota. They worked as missionaries in Liberia, China, the Philippines, and Brazil. They were directors of religious education in big parishes and social workers in inner-city slums. They lived in mountain huts and primitive fishing camps. They cared for the sick and the poor, helped at childbirth and buried the dead, worked as registered nurses and certified teachers. They taught the Bible and under the most exhausting and crude circumstances witnessed to Jesus Christ as Lord and Savior.

In the eighty-six years of its existence, 1885 through 1970, the order of deaconesses in the Episcopal Church attracted almost five hundred women. In many dioceses it was a vital, important ministry to the poor and sick. In its last years the order faded, no longer popular as a special ministry for women, and fell victim to the changing roles, opportunities, and aspirations of women beginning to seek equality with men in the church and in society. In its last decade only two or three ordinations took place every year, and a few of the remaining deaconesses eventually became priests. The last woman ordained deaconess, on 20 September 1970, was Shirley Woods, who became a priest in 1977 and was dean of the

41

✳

School for Deacons in the diocese of California until she retired in 1990.

## PERPETUAL DEACONS

After World War II the Episcopal Church grew rapidly in membership. To satisfy the need for sacramental and pastoral assistance in parishes, General Convention in 1952 restored the diaconate for men, commonly called "perpetual deacons" (the term used in the marginal description in the canons). The 1952 canon describes this deacon as

> a man of devout character and proved fitness, desirous to serve in the capacity of Deacon without relinquishing his secular occupation and with no intention of seeking advancement to the Priesthood . . . [I.34. 10(a)]

He must be at least thirty-two years old. Candidacy lasts at least six months. He is examined in a list of subjects, but educational requirements are lower than those for the priesthood. The deacon "shall exercise his Ministry as assistant in any parish or parishes to which, at the request or with the consent of the Rector and Vestry, he may be assigned by the Ecclesiastical Authority," but may not be in charge of a congregation. A final clause provides for a deacon "who may afterward desire to be advanced to the Priesthood." An amendment in 1964 allowed the deacon to be in charge of a congregation under certain circumstances. In 1967 an amendment provided modifications of the educational requirements for an indigenous deacon.

The provision for perpetual deacons was moderately popular. From 1952 through 1970, when canonical changes introduced women deacons and altered the nature of the order, 517 men were ordained under the canon. Most were ordained in a few dioceses such as Michigan and California (where Bishop James A. Pike preferred to ordain groups of deacons just before Christmas each year). Most were older men, raised out of the congregations in which they were to function as deacon, often personally picked by the parish priest, and locally trained. Actually, the ordination statistics are misleadingly low, because male deacons of the perpetual type—curates, or sacramental and pastoral assistants—continued

42
❋

to be ordained after 1970, but with decreasing frequency, and after 1980 it was a rare bishop who ordained an old-style deacon for ministry solely within the congregation.

At their best, perpetual deacons stayed close to the people and found their ministry in visiting the sick and needy of the parish and bringing them the sacrament. Rectors came and went, but the deacon remained, a perpetual curate. A good example of this is found in a novel entitled *The Deacon*, written by a perpetual deacon, Robert E. Gard of Wisconsin.[12] In the story a deacon narrates a tale about the ghost of Bishop Jackson Kemper, the famous missionary in that part of the country, who benevolently haunts Grace Church in Madison (a parish famous in the liturgical movement), and with the help of the sexton, a crotchety, lovable but slightly dotty octogenarian, endeavors to save the church building from the evil forces of progress. The building loses, the ghost fades, but the apostolic tradition endures. The deacon in the novel symbolizes two values in the parish, mediation and continuity. He is "a bridge figure," ordained yet remaining a layman in lifestyle, who over the years has become "a listening post for many," especially the old. He is also permanent. "A priest can be replaced; a deacon, in evidence at the same altar for twenty, thirty, forty years, assisting so many people, cannot."

But not all the perpetual deacons after 1970 were as content and loved as Gard was. Many were unhappy, feeling rejected by the church and betrayed by changes that left them marooned in the past. About twenty years ago I received a sad letter from an elderly deacon in Tennessee, whose wife had died, and who lamented, "They have taken away my ministry!" He meant that he could no longer pass the chalice, for his rector had given his chalice to licensed eucharistic ministers. The church had given the deacon no support in the loss of his wife or his ministry, and had made no effort to help an old deacon find new service in a new age.

Sometimes deacons' unhappiness is their own fault. One criticism of perpetual deacons was their occasional excess of sacramental zeal. Because the 1928 Book of Common Prayer, whatever its historic and literary virtues, was strangely mute about diaconal liturgy, deacons had to invent a good deal. In most places perpetual deacons officiated at the "deacon's mass"—a public communion service using the reserved sacrament (for which there was no rubrical provision)—and some deacons went so far as to say part of the eucharistic prayer, sometimes stopping after the Sanctus, sometimes omitting only the words of institution. To bring order out of disorderly behavior, the 1979 Book of Common Prayer provided rubrics for such a liturgy and required the deacon to omit the entire eucharistic prayer and fraction. Even after 1979, many older deacons mistakenly treated the "deacon's mass" as a regular form of liturgy, rather than as an emergency feeding from the cupboard.

Other critics have charged that perpetual deacons were trying to take a shortcut into the priesthood. Indeed, some did go on to priestly orders, as the canon permitted. Without tracking the biographical records of all 517 perpetual deacons ordained in 1952 through 1970, it is hard to tell exactly how many became priests. An inspection of the published ordination reports indicates that only four became priests within a year or two of their deaconing. Others became priests years later, mainly during the tumultuous 1970s. Who knows how many! Given the large number of perpetual deacons still alive in 1990, I suspect they were few. Let us remember that the bishop urged or allowed them to become priests. Some were missionary or indigenous deacons whom the church intended to make priests. Some discerned a new call. Some were persuaded by the bishop or others. A few took the easy path. In main, though, the canon was used for what it was designed, deacons until death.

So let us honor the perpetual deacons. For almost two decades, maybe longer, the church needed them and ordained them. Most of them ministered with dedication and did not aspire to "higher office." They loved the church they served, the people they served, the altar they served. But the need for them had passed.

44

✳

# EPISCOPAL CHURCH:
# CONTEMPORARY DEACONS

The three early waves of the diaconate in the Episcopal Church have vanished, as the church's needs for ministry have changed. Mission areas need indigenous priestly leadership, as well as deacons who encourage and lead the people in ministry. As fully recognized members of an historic order, women are a vital part of the ministry of deacons. The sacramental and pastoral ministries of perpetual deacons have become absorbed in the rising perception of baptismal ministry as the obligation of all the faithful.

45
✳

The early waves, however, have much to tell us. They teach that diaconal leadership should be local and daring. Like William West Skiles, deacons serve when they are part of the culture in which they labor. Like David Oakerhater, deacons serve when they can say, "You all know me, you remember when I . . ." The local Christians should select deacons out of their midst and support them as members of the assembly with a special role. Like Milnor Jones, deacons serve when they dare, when they speak out and act out, when they get themselves and others in trouble—even when they arouse the mob.

The early waves teach us, too, that the inclusion of women in holy orders is too important to be compromised and weakened by obsolete attitudes about women's place in church and society. Women have breathed new life into the diaconate. Women deacons have succeeded as outward and visible signs of ministry—especially to the sick and the poor—and a diaconate without women would be incomplete and sadly deprived. I could say the same about others, those sometimes regarded as inferior, whom the church excludes from ordained leadership.

They teach us also that close pastoral association with local Christians over a long time benefits both the church and the deacon. In this unpredictable world we may scorn permanence, but stability strengthens the church—as it strengthens the home and family. The people of God who formerly welcomed the stranger value friendship over estrangement. And the local people are more likely to follow a familiar deacon than a distant one into service in the world.

## THE 1970S: A TRANSITIONAL DECADE

In 1971 the Episcopal Church began to ordain a new style of deacon, in what was actually an attempt to recover an old style—the classic diaconate of the early church. A few years earlier, in the Roman Catholic Church, Vatican II had called for this recovery in the form of a permanent diaconate, which Paul VI promulgated in 1967. The Lambeth Conference of 1968 had urged Anglican churches to open the order to men and women in ordinary life. Liturgical trial in the Episcopal Church, leading eventually to the 1979 Book of Common Prayer, included deacons and other baptized persons as vital parts of a diversified liturgy. Women could be deacons. Most important, the Episcopal Church began to expect deacons to function directly under the bishop as symbols of the servant Christ and as special servants of the poor in the world.

During the same decade, many men used the deacon canon to become priests, and many dioceses allowed and even supported this legal but peripheral use of the canon. The 1973–78 bulge in the number of male deacons ordained priests coincided with the movement to ordain women as priests, as well as with a trend toward ordaining older men as priests. Perhaps these men who followed the deacon track to become priests wanted to avoid the economic and social disruption of seminary. Perhaps they lacked confidence in the Episcopal Church's support of its deacons, or perhaps they simply viewed the diaconate as a transitional period and the priesthood as the ordained norm. The answer may lie in a complex set of concurrent events, but the trend was disturbing. For six years the Episcopal Church seemed unwilling to order itself for *diakonia*, and in general the ordering of the church itself appeared confused and unruly.

The stories of several deacons ordained during the 1970s, mine among them, illustrate the transitional nature of the diaconate during that decade. We were sometimes confused about what we were and where we belonged. Many of us had to find our own way without the help or guidance of our bishops, who tended to be puzzled by our desire to become deacons. The old perpetual diaconate often cast its shadow over our vocations.

In 1970, under the influence partly of the liturgical movement and partly of the Roman Catholic revival of the order, I applied for the diaconate in the diocese of Louisiana. My bishop, Iveson Noland, who would let people do whatever they wanted so long as it appeared "catholic," cheerfully allowed me to proceed. After a year of solitary "reading for orders" to prepare for canonical examinations, I took the same exams as the seminary graduates. I sat for my formal photograph in clerical dress. At my ordination on 11 July 1971 Bishop Noland stood in the pulpit and addressed me as "Father Plater, the new curate of St. Anna's." The next day, in clerical dress, I drove to the airport to pick up a visitor, and the parking lot attendant waved me out without payment. A week later I received a clergy discount at a clothing store. But when an Episcopal school offered me a job as chaplain, members of the board of trustees turned me down on the grounds that I wasn't "fully ordained."

As it turned out, my ministry as deacon took a far different course. It led me first to the local prison, then to hospitals, and then to the surgical wards in New Orleans Charity Hospital, where many of the patients are the gunshot and stabbing casualties of urban warfare. In the parish I visited the sick and shut-in, and in the diocese I served as secretary of the commission on ministry and as a coordinator of lay hospital visiting. Finally, in 1998 the bishop named me archdeacon, directing the diaconate program and assisting him in vocations and liturgy. Farther afield I have a ministry of editing, writing, and speaking. Recently I estimated that I have undergone about fifteen major changes in ministry in more than thirty years; the bishop called me to half the changes, and the other half I started on my own.

Perhaps more typical of the transitional decade are the stories of women who either stumbled into or were talked into the diaconate.

47

✳

Phina Borgeson "went to seminary because I wanted to go back to school, and it was the only generalist professional degree."

> When I was at seminary, my inner call came through a study of the proposed ordination rites. The phrase "to interpret to the church" really hit me right between the eyes. My call was confirmed through my work with the people of the Diocese of Nevada at our summer camp, Galilee. I was told by women leading the movement for the ordination of women to the presbyterate and the episcopacy that it was pointless to want to be a deacon, because the power in the church lay with being a priest or a lay leader, preferably wealthy. A few professors and fellow students heard what I was saying about the diaconate, and helped me ground my theology, and create, in the free wheeling early seventies, a curriculum that was appropriate to my gifts and vocation.

Borgeson was ordained in 1974 by Wesley Frensdorff, who put her in charge of ministry development in a diocese now famous for its expression of "total ministry." She remained in that job for fourteen years and later served as Christian education missioner for the Diocese of Los Angeles. Borgeson finds the experience of seeking church employment contradictory and frustrating; deacons are often hired and turned down for reasons unrelated to capability. She now earns a living combining work for a non-profit organization with church consulting, trying to exercise her diaconal gifts of teaching, administration, and preaching on the margins of the church and society. "I see servant leadership as focusing on enabling others to serve," she writes, "And I see servanthood as more a style of ministry than a particular set of duties."

Borgeson recognizes that being a deacon is a risky business, which not only places the deacon in jeopardy, but also poses a terrible threat to those who wish to defend the church as it currently exists. "And whenever you threaten, you've got to expect some pain, most of it seemingly undeserved. My problem is, I just don't know how to do it any differently if Jesus is our example."[1]

In 1977 Borgeson preached at the ordination of several seminary graduates, to a congregation including Arlinda Cosby, who had begun to feel vocationally different from her classmates at the

48

Church Divinity School of the Pacific. "Her words seemed to turn on a light bulb somewhere. Eureka! That's it!" Momentarily stalled by pregnancy and the birth of a daughter, Cosby graduated and was ordained in 1979 to find herself with a young child, a permanently disabled husband, and a desire to work in institutions offering long-term care. Her bishop, her rector, and an archdeacon advised her to forget about earning a living in the church. "One of them said I had three strikes against me: I was a woman, I was a deacon, and I wanted to work with the elderly." She worked for a while as activity director in a convalescent hospital but became frustrated at trying to justify this position as service of Christ.

Eventually, in 1981, the deanery in Alameda, California, hired Cosby to coordinate the ministry of twenty-two congregations to seven thousand patients in nearly a hundred facilities. She has been at this job ever since, with a vision "to initiate, support, and strengthen the ministries of our local Episcopal congregations to the convalescent hospitals in their communities, offering training, education, support to clergy and the laity, and pastoral care for families and staff as well as patients." In this position, working three-quarters time and paid the diocesan minimum for a vicar, Cosby works hard to satisfy overwhelming needs, often despairs over the dearth of volunteers, and tries to develop some kind of relationship with the three parishes in which she functions liturgically. She does not feel close to the other deacons of the diocese, most of whom are graduates of the diocesan School for Deacons, which troubles her at times. "Feeling neither fish nor fowl has become a familiar feeling . . . perhaps it's only what life on the diaconal edge is all about."

More typical of the decade was the call of Jean Brooks of Vermont. Around 1972 her priest suggested that she become a deacon. At first she regarded him as mildly deranged, but the idea kept resurfacing, and "it dawned on me that this invitation might be a way that God had prepared for me to return thanks for a long ago life-changing conversion experience." Her bishop, also skeptical but "willing to be shown," ordained her in 1979.

> I myself couldn't be very persuasive on the matter since
> I had scarcely any idea what a deacon was or did. My
> preparation did nothing to enlighten me about the dia-
> conate, since it was not designed for that purpose. After

49
✳

three years of preparation and taking the General
Ordination Examinations, I made my final appearance
before the Commission on Ministry. When asked what I
expected to be doing as a deacon, I recall that my answer
was: "I suppose I will be doing whatever David [her priest]
tells me to do." I don't think anyone on the Commission
had any more idea about diaconal ministry than I did,
in fact possibly less, and I suppose I sounded nicely
biddable, so they passed me on.

Her experience as a deacon became "a continuous unfolding of
opportunities for learning and service," all arising from needs unrelated to any structure or regulation. Administering a discretionary
fund, she cared for the parish needy, and her outreach to the community involved organizations related to the hungry, the developmentally disabled, emotionally disturbed children and adults, and
prisoners. She often enlisted "eager and dedicated young people in
these situations."

The decade of the 1970s was also a time of serious canonical
revision in attempts to bring about reform. Thus in 1970 General
Convention enacted significant changes in the old perpetual deacon
canon, resulting in a new canon that begins:

A man of Christian character, proven fitness, and leadership in his community, who is willing to serve in the capacity of Deacon without relinquishing his secular occupation, may be proposed and recommended to the Bishop,
for enrollment as a Postulant, by the Minister and Vestry
of the Parish in which his service is desired . . . .

The drafters, principally H. Boone Porter, intended the canon to
restore the diaconate as a permanent order with local ties.
Originally for deacons only, the canon was afterwards expanded to
provide for subsequent ordination to the priesthood. Alaska and
similar dioceses with remote and ethnic congregations needed local
priests, or sacramentalists (as they were then called), and Canon
III.10.10 seemed the easiest way to get them.

The canon also required a major change in practice, for prospec-
tive deacons were no longer to apply on their own initiative. Under
the canon a qualified person is to be "proposed and recommended

to the Bishop" by a parish, mission, or diocesan body. This provision was meant to shift the emphasis on God's call from the person to the community, from the inner call to the outer call. The proposed deacon had to be willing (but was not required) to remain in secular work. Although a few deacons ordained under this canon received stipends from the church, at least for part-time work, most remained non-stipendiary.

Several important amendments were made over the next nine years. In 1973 the paragraph on preparation for ordination was amended to introduce some flexibility, and consequently preparation was divided into two equal parts, academic and practical, thus shifting the emphasis from solely academic study (often modeled after seminary preparation) to include practical training and recognition of the value of practical experience. The canon also required "an evaluation of the Candidate's attainments" instead of the usual formal examinations. The sum of these changes implied a new kind of deacon, formed more in the hospitals, prisons, and soup kitchens than in the study hall.

As in the early church, deacons were subject to the bishop. The bishop assigned them, and they could not accept work in another diocese without the consent of the bishops of both dioceses. Unfortunately, the canons assumed that all deacons were the same, as though there were no difference between "permanent" and "transitional" deacons, although trends in the diaconate were leading toward two distinctive types of deacons.

The 1970s were years of uncertainty, upheaval, and often chaos. Many in the church held desperately to old and tried ways, while others were eager to try anything new. The resulting tumult applied to orders as well as to liturgy and other aspects of church life. Until the 1980s few bishops and commissions on ministry took seriously either the canonical requirement that deacons be "proposed and recommended" or the requirement for practical training. For a few years the revival of the diaconate seemed in danger of collapse. Confusion about the role of the deacon was a large part of the problem.

After 1979 the transitional period ended. Holy orders began to recover a measure of harmony, and service of "the poor, the weak, the sick, and the lonely," as the prayer book directed, rose in significance as the distinguishing mark of the diaconate. The new Book of Common Prayer assigned deacons a central role in the life of the church. Canon III.10.10 began to be used for what it was primarily intended—the ordination of deacons who would remain in the order.

During these same years the deacons of the Episcopal Church and their friends built an organization. After 1970 the Central House for Deaconesses, located in an old house at 1914 Orrington Avenue in Evanston, Illinois, lost its purpose as a training center for women. Its director, Frances Zielinski, a former deaconess become deacon, decided to expand the organization to include men deacons. In 1974 the board of trustees, which now included several men deacons as well as women deacons, changed the name to the National Center for the Diaconate.

The Center had a troubled start. One problem was lack of money; another was lack of energy and direction. Semi-annual meetings were poorly attended, brief, and listless. Trustees traveled often hundreds of miles to attend meetings one to two hours long. Projects were vague and seldom carried out. Some board members complained. Some stayed away. The Center had little sense of what to do. Its one important activity in the mid-1970s was a survey of some thousand deacons (permanent and transitional) over two years. The survey found that deacons whose diaconate centered on the altar tended to feel frustrated and as a result often sought the priesthood. By contrast those whose diaconate centered on ministry to the poor and needy tended to feel fulfilled and excited and were content to remain deacons.

The first new work, approved in 1977, was the Deaconess History Project, a worthwhile activity, which needed support but which turned out to be a major drain on funds. The second was a small newsletter, *Diakoneo*, which in 1978 began to be published quarterly and mailed free to deacons and friends.

The turning point can be traced to the efforts of two people. One was James L. Lowery Jr., a priest in Boston, who for six and a half years traveled the country in the course of his consulting work and spoke to diocese after diocese about his theory of the four waves of the diaconate. He also described the basic four-part design of a diaconate program: selection, training, deployment, and supervision and support. The other friend was Wesley Frensdorff, bishop of Nevada. When Frensdorff joined the board in 1978, the Center began to come alive. At his second meeting he started a discussion about the theology of the diaconate, and the meeting lasted an unprecedented five hours. Frensdorff expressed his dream of a deacon in every parish as an outward and visible sign of servant ministry and as an enabler of the ministry of all the baptized.

Elected president in 1983, Frensdorff brought several strengths to the center. One was a theological approach. He argued that deacons are not merely functionaries; they fill a sacramental role as symbols or icons of Christ. Another strength was experience. Frensdorff had already put into practice in Nevada his concept of "total ministry," whereby a parish or mission organizes itself for the ministry of all the baptized. Total ministry includes selection by the congregation, from its members, of its presbyter and deacon—perhaps several of each.

The National Center for the Diaconate continued to be plagued by financial setbacks. Out of a desire to include the Anglican Church of Canada, which was seeking to renew the diaconate, the North American Association for the Diaconate came into being in 1986 as its replacement. One activity of both organizations was to hold or cosponsor conferences. The first three, in 1979, 1981, and 1984, were characterized by the uncertainty over the diaconate that still was widespread in the Episcopal Church.[2] Many deacons and persons in the application process came to the conferences seeking emotional support. Some shared tales of woe; others were in pain over what they perceived as their bishops' neglect. At the 1984 conference several deacons openly disagreed over the propriety of clerical dress for their order. Some opposed clerical dress and titles for deacons. Some defended the clerical collar. More in tune with the aggressive new style of deacon, as with the American trait of self-reliance, was a motto suggested at the 1981 meeting by William B. Arnold, a deacon in Central Florida: "Don't ask, do it!" The motto also suggested a mood of rebellion against bishops.

A similar mood characterized the 1987 conference on the diaconate held in Kansas City, Missouri. The Presiding Bishop of the Episcopal Church, Edmond L. Browning, pledged to encourage the diaconate in the Episcopal Church, but also challenged deacons to articulate and model diaconal ministry, to join him in making the church inclusive, and to re-examine the spiritual basis of their ministry. In the question session the next day, however, Browning faced heavy opposition from several deacons and others to the continued use of the transitional diaconate—what one deacon called "climbing up a ladder." Browning argued in return that the transitional

53
✳

diaconate should be emphasized as "a spiritual moment in the life of a person who's come into the ordained ministry." This depiction of permanent office as fleeting experience stirred up a nest of hornets. Sarah Tracy, who formed deacons in Northern Indiana (where she was later archdeacon), charged, "The deacon, the honest-to-God deacon, is trained to be a deacon. The transitional deacon is trained to be a priest, and they are giving *diakonia* a bad name."[3]

Another organization involved in the renewal of the diaconate was Associated Parishes for Liturgy and Mission. Founded in 1946, in its early years Associated Parishes campaigned for catholic liturgical principles, especially the recovery of the Eucharist as the central act of Christian worship. In 1977 the council of the organization turned its attention to the diaconate and issued the Wewoka Statement, calling for

> the renewal of the order of deacons as a full, normal ministry in the Church, alongside the priesthood. The diaconate is not properly a stepping-stone or a back door to the priesthood. It is not an auxiliary ministry. Deacons and priests have equal but different ministries whose functions are clearly outlined in the new ordinal of the Proposed Book of Common Prayer.

The council also urged that candidates be ordained directly to the priesthood, without an intervening transitional diaconate, and that deacons "be eligible to be elected as bishop and ordained directly to that order."[4] This was the main issue raised by the Wewoka Statement—*per saltum* ("by a leap"), or direct ordination, the ancient practice of ordaining a person directly to the order intended. Despite extensive overhauls of the canons on ministry in 1988 and 2003, ordination to the priesthood still requires prior ordination to the diaconate. The Episcopal Church thus leaves unresolved one of its greatest contradictions. The 1979 Book of Common Prayer makes no mention of holding or remaining in a prior order, and all ordinands approach the bishop vested in a white garment without stole or vestment of office. The symbolism of the liturgy says that instead of asserting prior office (whether they continue in one is unclear) they come to ordination simply as baptized persons.

## MATURITY IN THE PAST GENERATION

The 1980s were a time of increased public discussion of the order. James M. Barnett's scholarly study *The Diaconate: A Full and Equal Order* in 1981 helped the church take the diaconate seriously as a permanent order of ministry. Furthermore, through its revision of the canons on ministry in 1988, the Episcopal Church began to separate the diaconate from the priesthood—but only in part. The process for recruitment and selection, postulancy, and candidacy was shared, without distinction, by deacons and priests. The former description of a deacon's qualifications—"A person of Christian character, proven fitness, and leadership in his community"—no longer appeared in the canons, while the "proposal" process of the old deacon canon now applied to both deacons and priests. The main difference lay in formation and in the final steps of the ordination process. Formation was still divided into two parts, academic and practical. Deacons were assigned to a parish or mission "at the request, or with the consent," of the rector and vestry. A deacon who moved to another diocese might be given a "license" to function as deacon only on the written request of the bishop, with the written consent of the standing committee.

A story told by Canadian deacon Maylanne Maybee at a conference in 1989 shows a change in the nature of deacons. A woman on the bank of a river sees someone drowning. The woman jumps in and saves the person. A few minutes later, she sees someone else drowning and jumps in again. This happens again, and it happens a few more times. Finally the woman walks away, and the crowd that has gathered asks where she is going. "You can't leave these people to drown!" She answers, "I'm going up the river to see who's throwing them in."

Deacons ordained in the 1980s tended to look for the sources of drowning; some of them also experienced it. One of these was Marcos Rivera, ordained in Central Florida in 1987. Two years later he attended an ecumenical conference on *diakonia* in Kingston, Jamaica, of which he wrote: "My native background and lifestyle in a tropical area did little to prepare me for the food delicacies, weather, scenery, and breathtaking beauty of Jamaica. Neither was I prepared for the poverty in such a beautiful place." Rivera came from a background exotic in its own way. Born in Puerto Rico in 1939, he grew up in the slums of New York, where he became a heroin addict and for thirteen years was a member of street gangs. Then, converted to Christ, spiritually and physically delivered from gang violence, street life, and drug dependence, he left New York, attended college in Ohio, founded three homes for boys there, and eventually settled in Florida. In 1974 he set up Anchor House, a home for neglected and abused boys, which he still runs as executive director.

At the Jamaica meeting, attended mostly by deaconesses and other women from protestant churches, Rivera listened while speaker after speaker talked about God as a woman and prayed to God as "Mother." Finally he rose and told the audience that street people like him were not interested in the sex of God, or even in God. Later a group of women followed him out of the hall and thanked him for his comments.

Rivera has a strong sense of the power of Christ to change lives and of the presence of Christ in men, women, and children suffering from poverty. Like Francis of Assisi, he often finds in commonplace experience the dramatic physical evidence of God. "While walking inside a mission for the handicapped," he writes of his Jamaican trip, "I was approached by a young woman of indeterminable age. She grabbed my hand and kissed it. As she kissed my hand, she also reached and hugged me. I felt a fiery sensation through my entire body. I have never been a mystic, but when she hugged me I felt as though I was being hugged by the Lord. A transformation occurred within me."[5]

Justus Van Houten came home from Vietnam in 1973 with a desire to become a Franciscan friar. At the time he felt that the vocation of friar was incompatible with the vocation of deacon (although Francis of Assisi had been a deacon). In the early 1980s, after ten years as a friar, he changed his mind and with the support of his brothers was ordained at the annual chapter of the Society of St. Francis in 1986, as the society's first deacon friar. "The community felt that it needed to have the servant aspect of their ministry sacramentalized."

For the first two years as deacon, Brother Justus worked for the San Francisco Night Ministry, a job that entailed spending Saturday nights on the streets, in bars and coffee shops, and other places where people hang out. He helped and befriended robbed tourists, stranded people, patients who had lost their medication, recovering alcoholics, and potential suicides. One night the patrons of a seedy gay bar decided to stage a drag show to cover the burial expenses of "Diane," a bartender who had died from AIDS. Justus attended as a sign of the church's official presence. When the sound system failed to arrive, the crowd became restless, and someone asked him to do a memorial service. "I talked about love. The love that was so obvious for so many people to have come out to raise money for Diane's burial, and that while I didn't know Diane's religious background, that as a Christian who believed in a God of love, that this outpouring of love helped me to have a deeper understanding of God as I knew him. We ended with a toast to Love and passed the hat."

Some weeks later, during a routine visit at the county jail, an inmate told Justus that the service for Diane had been his first encounter with a church that did not judge and condemn him. The inmate was later baptized in the jail, "quite a courageous act on his part."

Montie Slusher retired in 1990 as a teacher with the North Slope Borough School District in Barrow, on the Arctic coast of Alaska, and moved inland to Fairbanks. His ministry in one of the coldest and remotest parts of the continent began with his arrival in 1969 to work with the poor and those who needed education and vocational training. Raised as a Methodist, he attended a nearby Episcopal church, was confirmed, and served as lay reader and senior warden. "The deacons' charge to interpret to the church the needs of the world was very real to me, as I worked with those who had such needs." As school principal in the small village of Point Lay, where about half the 120 residents were Episcopalians, he learned more about the diaconate and was ordained in 1985.

Slusher spends his retirement working as a deacon. The bishop asked him to put his experiences as social worker, educator, and vocational trainer into writing grants and training local people for native ministries in the interior and Arctic coast. This direction from his bishop is important to Slusher, who believes that "diaconal ministry is only possible with the guidance of the bishop." His background as teacher and deacon also leads him to emphasize the connection between ordinary life and the church. He writes:

> The deacon's journey is not an upward movement, but
> rather one of lateral movement into the world of people.
> The deacon must lead others from worship back into the

day-by-day realities all must face in the world. If a deacon
feels he has "arrived," he will become frustrated or worse
yet, stale. The role of the deacon is to see that the draw-
bridge is always open allowing entry into the castle and
that two way traffic is possible allowing entry into the
castle (church) and to lead others back into the world.

In 1982, four months after ordination, Shep Jenks quit his job
and, surviving on Navy retirement pay, went to work as a deacon in
the diocese of California:

I was assigned first to one mission church and then to
another where my bishop felt that help was needed. I
worked hard and did well. I was really filling a position as
an unpaid curate (or assistant vicar). I was on a high. My
prayer life was good. I read and studied Holy Scriptures
regularly. I had recovered from a divorce and found Nancy,
who is a born servant. I had a disagreement with the vicar
and handled it poorly. I had to be right. The naval officer
(and all the power that entailed) came out.

The bishop moved Jenks into San Francisco to help at Canon
Kip Community Center, where he ended up as executive director,
unpaid, working overtime, "and thoroughly rewarded personally as
Nancy's and my new ministry flourished." Having started as a
curate, he came to believe that deacons should be "down in the
bowels of the inner city."

I now feel that a deacon can best serve (as a symbol of
the need for a servant church) when the person serves
in the world but with the laity of a parish/mission. It is
most discouraging to be in a place where either priests
or bishops can do it all or in which the need for servanthood is not envisioned.

Gloria E. Wheeler, ordained in Central Florida in 1983, developed a ministry of healing, which included the personal experienc-
ing of miracles as a result of prayer. But her work as deacon
also ranged from "balancing checkbooks for the aged to emptying
urinals for a bedridden bishop." Her husband, Robert, strongly

supported her ministry, which involved being a woman deacon in a conservative diocese. When she was seeking ordination in the Cathedral of St. Luke in Orlando, "it was then ludicrous to even think of women in the sanctuary unless they were Altar Guild members." As one result of her visibility as deacon, the diocese saw opportunities for ordained women in the diocese.

Jeffrey Ferguson of Maine found her ministry undergoing a drastic change during the process leading to ordination in 1985. She first envisioned herself as a parish assistant, working with young persons and perhaps visiting in nursing homes, but while taking clinical pastoral education in preparation for the diaconate she found herself in a prison for men. "From the moment I entered the gates for my interview I knew I was where I belonged." There she stayed for six years as an assistant chaplain, visiting inmates twelve hours a week.

> What a growing period this was for me. The inmates
> challenged me daily with questions about Scripture,
> God, sin, Satan, and Jesus. They pushed me to read and
> study the Bible as I had never done in order to be able
> to talk with them. They brought out my ignorance of our
> judicial, educational, and welfare systems. And they raised
> the fighter in me. I'm slowly but surely becoming a chal-
> lenger of each of these services or systems. . . . The inmates
> challenged me to enter their pain and sorrow. This put
> a large burden on me as I had always kept my emotions
> under control, to myself. As I learned to enter their world
> I found myself freed to share my own pain and more espe-
> cially my joy in the gifts of God. This too was a turning
> point for many of the men when they realized that other
> people too, perhaps especially chaplains, had pains and
> sorrows and yet could meet our Lord with joy.

In 1989 Ferguson's ministry took another direction. When she told her bishop that she was ready to leave prison work, he assigned her to move three hundred miles to the northernmost county of Maine, form a cluster council for five churches, and act as a consultant in the search for a priest. A year later, the task was complete and she returned home, back to prison work. Ferguson finds that "I walk more closely with our Lord and speak of him more often and more freely. I believe I am more adept at noticing hidden emotions, particularly pain, sorrow, and anger. The Holy Bible has become a never ending source of information, anecdotes, refreshment, and renewal as I become more familiar with it. I find joy in all my work even as I steel myself to speak out about injustice and abusive behavior."

Bonnie Polley describes herself as "a Cajun living in Glitter Gulch." As a child growing up in Lake Charles, Louisiana, she liked to visit her daddy's law office next door to the jail, stand outside looking up at the men in the jail window, and tell herself, "If only those people had anybody to talk to they would probably not be so bad." As a grownup in Las Vegas, Nevada, she went inside the county jail and listened. Her parish called her to the diaconate, and she was ordained in 1982. After twenty-one years as a volunteer chaplain at the Clark County Detention Center, she was put on the payroll.

> I might find myself cashing checks, picking up mail, contacting a family member, providing reading glasses, replacing a hearing-aid battery. The list of requests is endless. The funniest request I think I ever had was to go and feed this man's horse that had been left out in the desert when the man was arrested. In asking particulars about the situation, the man told me that the horse was afraid of people, would bite, and that was why he could not get his friend to go feed him. I asked him how he could be sure that the horse would not bite me and his reply was that I had a direct line upstairs. I said that I wondered if the horse knew that. The end result was that we found someone to take care of the horse and the man was relieved of his anxiety about his horse. With tears in his eyes the man told me that there really must be a God because I cared enough to help him, and if I cared then maybe God cared.

One of only a handful of persons ever to enter seminary for the diaconate, Vicki Black found that Nashotah House helped to confirm her calling. It also helped her "to understand that God was calling me to be a deacon who worked in cooperation with people in different yet equal ministries, and not 'just a deacon,' assisting a priest in his or her more elevated calling within a hierarchical order of ministries." Following her ordination in 1987, her bishop assigned her to a parish, put her in charge of retreats and conferences at DeKoven Center, and asked her to help administer the new catechumenal process in the diocese.

In the midst of making phone calls, typing schedules, welcoming guests, publishing brochures and newsletters, and assisting in liturgies, Vicki struggled to balance frantic activity with authentic ministry. She found time to hold up "the importance of spirituality to an institutional church which in its rush towards programming has all too often lost its ability to value spiritual growth as an essential aspect of the Christian life." She searched for a spirituality of servanthood in a culture that "tells us (especially women) that we are to 'set our boundaries,' not to let others take advantage of us, not to accept menial tasks unless others are doing as many of those tasks as we are."

After moving to Massachusetts in the early 1990s, Vicki focused on a ministry of the written word and has been working as an editor and designer in religious publishing ever since. She sees a strong parallel between being a book editor and being a deacon at the altar. Both roles, she believes, are helping to serve nourishment to others. At the altar deacons help to prepare and distribute the bread and wine of the Eucharist, while deacons who endeavor to prepare books on spirituality and theology help to offer the spiritual food of the Word. Vicki also understands her editorial work to be a way of living out the traditional diaconal ministry of being an interpreter, as she seeks to give voice to the author's ideas by making words as strong and clear as possible, and to reflect back to the author the needs and concerns of those who will read the book.

These stories of deacons ordained in the 1970s and 80s illustrate a ministry in the process of evolution. The modern deacon saves the drowning but also finds the causes and tells the church about them, returning to the gathered people of God and around the altar enacting the diaconal ministry. While serving the poor in the broadest sense, this deacon also seeks to define the diaconate in terms an expanded ministry of action, word, and liturgy, functioning within the local people of God and in close cooperation with the bishop of the diocese. It is clear that for many deacons the encouragement, guidance, and direct involvement of their bishop have become highly important factors in their ministry.

61

*

The major story of recent years has been the discovery of bishops. Within the contemporary diaconate we can discern three stages, in a rough and often overlapping sequence. In the first stage, mainly in the 1970s and early 80s, deacons moved out of the church and into the world, giving personal care to God's poor. In the second, in the late 1980s and early 90s, deacons returned to the church and gathered or encouraged the faithful for ministry in the world. In the third, in the past decade, deacons reinvented the ancient concept of the deacon as bishop's agent, and in the process they found the virtue of diaconal community. These movements bore fruit, and were reflected, in new canon law on deacons, which General Convention enacted in 2003 (and which I describe in detail in Chapter 6).

Both bishops and deacons have profited from closer and more frequent contact. Bishops have begun to make time in frantic schedules to attend meetings of deacons, to pray with them, and to hear their stories. When deacons accompany bishops on their visitations to congregations, the liturgical and pastoral event takes on a new reality, and ministry acquires a different shape, less one-dimensional and more diverse and relational. By enacting their integral relationship, bishop and deacons show that the hierarchical ordering of the church is based, not on superiority and dominance, but on perfect harmony and unity.

CHAPTER FIVE

✳

# OTHER CHURCHES

The four waves in the Episcopal Church constitute one small part of the revival of the diaconate in the holy catholic church. In Canada and the rest of the Anglican Communion outside North America, and in other places and churches, the revival takes a different but related shape. Above all else it includes the experience and witness of several Roman Catholic priests imprisoned in Germany during World War II. Their reflection on the consequences of war and extermination has influenced the recovery of deacons in many churches besides their own.

63
✳

## THE ROMAN CATHOLIC CHURCH

The revival of the diaconate in the mid-twentieth century began in cellblock 26 of Dachau concentration camp. Roman Catholic priests, including Wilhelm Schamoni, and other Christian clerics interned there began to discuss secretly and at great risk how to revitalize the church after the war so that it would serve a crushed and defeated people in Europe. Their vision included the diaconate. Schamoni kept a written record of their discussions. His notes were smuggled out of the camp, and in 1947 Otto Pies, another priest in the camp, referred to them in an article. Fuller accounts were published later.[1]

These Dachau conversations had a profound effect on the Roman Catholic Church. In 1951 a young forest ranger, Hannes Kramer, formed the first *Diakonatskreis* (diaconate circle) of social workers in Freiburg who felt called to the diaconate, including their wives and fiancées. Other circles were formed in Germany and elsewhere, attracting the support of the theologian Karl Rahner, among others. After further public discussion and writing, Vatican II approved the proposal and Paul VI instituted the permanent diaconate. In a speech in the Vatican council, on 9 October 1964, Léon-Joseph Cardinal Suenens stressed the sacramental character of the diaconate as stemming from "supernatural realism" and added: "This grade seems to have been set up especially to provide direct help for the bishop in the care of the poor and the proper direction of the community," mainly in brotherly love and the breaking of the bread. He recommended that men already serving in diaconal ministries be ordained deacons.[2] By the end of 2001 there were 28,238 Roman Catholic permanent deacons in the world, all men, most of them married, with 13,000 in the United States. The Roman Catholic revival of the order is a vital part of the background of the revival in Anglican churches.

As the permanent diaconate of the Roman Catholic Church has developed over more than thirty years, its diocesan programs have adhered closely to the magisterium, or teaching authority of bishops, as declared in the decrees of Vatican II, papal statements, and curial and national guidelines. In the United States the permanent deacons, with their large numbers, have made many contacts with Episcopal deacons, and these connections are beneficial to both sides. Most Roman Catholic and Episcopal deacons share a strong commitment to works of mercy and justice in the world. Catholic deacons minister in all the familiar venues. They visit in hospitals and prisons. They feed the hungry, house the homeless, and comfort the dying. They emphasize the diaconal significance of Christian life in family, community, and workplace. And like all deacons they serve in parish liturgies. Episcopal deacons bring to the dialogue the experience of women as deacons, while Roman Catholic deacons bring the insight that one is just as much a deacon at home and on the job as in church on Sunday.

This ecumenical commonality sometimes leads to friendships and opportunities for learning and working together. In New Orleans every three years Catholic and Episcopal candidates study together in Clinical Pastoral Training (an adaptation of Clinical Pastoral Education), visiting prisons, hospitals, hospices, and other facilities and attending classes once a week.

The main differences between the Roman Catholic and the Episcopal diaconates lie in the area of marriage and women. The

Roman Catholic permanent diaconate is solely for men, and mainly for married men. Their wives usually take part in their training, approve and confirm their ordination, and often join their ministry as half of a diaconal team. Out of this union between orders and marriage has risen a theological concept in which the two sacraments intertwine. A wife extends her husband's diaconate, her husband extends their marriage into his diaconate, and thus the symbolic representation of Christ is multiplied. "A married diaconate takes people who in marriage have been successful at imaging the unity of Church and Christ and ordains them as other Christs."[3]

One mark of the Roman Catholic Church in the United States has been the willingness of its bishops to move deacons into positions of administrative responsibility. Deacons serve as directors of diaconate programs in most of the dioceses with healthy programs, and a deacon is appointed executive director of the Bishops' Committee on the Permanent Diaconate, headquartered in Washington.

Not all dioceses adhere to the vision once experienced at Dachau. In places with a severe shortage of priests, some Roman Catholic deacons are used as pastoral and sacramental assistants, taking on presidency functions, and hence they appear little different from priests. This expediency has proven harmful to the sacramental character of the diaconate.[4]

## THE ANGLICAN COMMUNION

In the Anglican Communion parallel but less dramatic influences have been at work. The first official expression of interest came as early as 1878 from the West Indian bishops, who suggested the possibility of deacons who remained in a secular calling, and whose educational background was lower than usually required. The feeling at Lambeth Conference 1878 was that only diocesan or provincial synods could establish this form of the diaconate. And there the matter rested until after World War II.

Every ten years the bishops of the entire Anglican Communion meet in England—at first at Lambeth Palace and then, when numbers became too great, mainly at the University of Kent in Canterbury—and it was at successive Lambeth conferences that they next took up the question of the diaconate. By the Lambeth meeting of 1958, the Episcopal Church had already revived the diaconate in the form of perpetual deacons. Recognizing this ordained ministry in North America, as well as the growing movement in Roman Catholicism to revive the order, Lambeth Conference 1958 made a tentative approach toward reviving the diaconate on a communion-wide basis.

A committee report, "The Order of Deacon," observed that in recent years the church had tended to emphasize the offices of reader and catechist at the expense of the diaconate. Either there is no place for the deacon, or else Anglicans must "give the office and function of a deacon its distinctive place, not only in the worship, but in the witness of the Church." The committee wanted Lambeth to invite each province in the Anglican Communion to discuss a revival of the distinctive diaconate, which then might include some commissioned lay ministries. The ordinal would have to be changed to include part-time workers, and this scheme would bring other legal, canonical, and constitutional difficulties.

On the basis of the committee report, Lambeth passed Resolution 88, "The Office of Deacon":

> The Conference recommends that each province of the Anglican Communion shall consider whether the office of Deacon shall be restored to its primitive place as a distinctive order in the Church, instead of being regarded as a probationary period for the priesthood.[5]

By the phrase "instead of," the bishops at Lambeth appear to have contemplated *replacing* the transitional diaconate with the order as anciently practiced. As we shall see, Anglican bishops and other representatives later backed away from this radical position.

Support for a restored diaconate was much stronger in 1968. It came initially in the form of a remarkable essay by John Howe, bishop of St. Andrews in Scotland and later secretary general of the Anglican Consultative Council. In his preparatory paper for Lambeth Conference 1968, "The Diaconate,"[6] Howe begins by reviewing the evidence of the diaconate in the New Testament, early church, and medieval and modern times. His brief historical survey, sound and full of insight, emphasizes the symbolic being of deacons rather than their diaconal functions or clerical status in the community. The responsibility of early deacons to carry humble loads in simple and lowly areas gave them a symbolic place related to Christ. The Seven of Acts 6, and the primitive deacons who followed them, were important not because they were clerics but because they performed humble service. In the early church the deacons even worked "as beachcombers who sought the corpses of mariners and provided decent burial." In time attention to status and liturgical function led to distortion of the diaconate. The medieval diaconate faded because the deacon could not celebrate mass—the distinctive function of the hierarchy in that age—and thus the diaconate had no purpose except as the final step on the road to priesthood. The Reformation did not change the practice of holy orders for the better. (The nineteenth-century revival of the deacon and deaconess in continental Lutheranism took place outside ordained ministry.) Now there is widespread concern to recover what Howe calls "a real diaconate."

In his essay Howe lists several main reasons for interest in the diaconate: criticism of the use of deacons in the churches today, ecumenical dialogue, nominal use of one of the three orders, shortage of clergy, and the need for assistance in the Eucharist. Of these reasons only the first three continue to be significant, at least in the Episcopal Church. But Howe cautions against a functional approach—that of setting up a diaconate to relieve a particular need. Instead, restoration should be based on "what the diaconate is and what deacons are for."

Howe places considerable emphasis on Acts 6 as a starting point that emphasizes flexibility, adaptability, God's powerful gift of grace in the ordained ministry, and the need for the church to display support for those carrying particular responsibilities. The present use of the diaconate as a final period before the priesthood receives no sanction from early history, and we should not confuse a transitional period of probation with a permanent order. Howe is one of the first to question those practices of training, status, and function (including collars and titles) that cause the diaconate to resemble the priesthood, observing that deacons must be distinct from both priests and lay ministers and not duplicate the ministry of either. He was also one of the first to challenge the concept of the indelibility of orders: Should the diaconate, at least, be indelible and lifelong or erasable and short-term?

Howe suggested three alternative courses of action for Lambeth 1968: (1) discard the diaconate, (2) discard the diaconate as a step to the priesthood but continue study and experiments, or (3) keep the present diaconate and continue to experiment. Howe clearly preferred the third course, and Lambeth 1968 agreed. But he also wanted to go further and identify the diaconate in existing lay ministries—catechists, readers, nurses, welfare workers, and secretaries—not to ordain them, but simply to commission and bless them with the laying on of hands. Training for such deacons would be diverse and appropriate to individual ministries. They would be commissioned in a simple service and licensed by the bishop for a specific ministry and term of years. "In most parts of the world, at such a making of deacons, complete simplicity and lack of trappings would be suitable." Howe closes his essay with a sentence that looks ahead to the new style of deacon:

> The familiar accompaniments of ordinations would too readily revive the curse of the diaconate—the withdrawal from the circumstances of lay life, and a restless feeling that it is not reason [sic] that they should serve tables, and that the Church should find some other men of good repute to appoint over that business.

Willing to restore the order of deacons, but not to the lengths of declericalization urged by Howe, the bishops at Lambeth 1968 addressed the issue in Resolution 32, "The Diaconate." First, the resolution recommended that a diaconate combining service of others with liturgical duties be open to men and women in secular occupations, full-time church workers, and those selected for the priesthood. Second, the resolution recommended that the ordinals should be revised to take this new role into account, to remove any suggestion that the diaconate is an inferior order, and to emphasize the elements of *diakonia* in the ministry of bishops and priests.[7]

The official report of Lambeth 1968 expands on this resolution. There the bishops argue that the practice of continuing to use the diaconate as a probationary period for priesthood is an ecumenical embarrassment (probably because it is untrue to Scripture) requiring reform. The diaconate, as part of Anglican tradition, should not be allowed to lapse, but should be given a more significant place within the Anglican Communion. The bishops recommend recovery and renewal of the diaconate, open to men and women and including both those professionally employed by the church and those in secular employment. Candidates for the priesthood should pass through and be part of the diaconate.

The mention in the resolution of "the continuing element of *diakonia* in the ministry of bishops and priests," a seemingly innocent phrase, may cause confusion today. One theological rationale for ordination to the diaconate of those intended for the priesthood has been that ordained priests need to be deacons to possess the fullness of diaconal ministry. Liturgical revision, occurring after 1968, has raised questions about the validity of such argument. Most modern Anglican baptismal rites, including those of the Episcopal Church and the Anglican Church of Canada, make it clear that a Christian receives both priesthood and *diakonia* (defined as loving service or *agape*) at baptism. To participate fully in Christian service all you need is to be baptized. The old career path of climbing from one order to another has washed away.

After the strong stand taken by Lambeth 1968, there was little left for the next conference to do. Not all the member churches were prompt to act on the ordination of women deacons, however, and Lambeth 1978 thought it desirable to pass a brief resolution on "Women in the Diaconate," which urges member churches to include women in the order.[8] The resolution reflected an action already taken in the General Convention of the Episcopal Church in 1970 (which also revised the canons for the diaconate in general). In the Church of England women were not ordained as deacons until February 1987. Aside from women as deacons, Lambeth 1978 paid no attention to the revival of the diaconate.

Actions on the diaconate were also taken at three meetings of the Anglican Consultative Council, or ACC, which was called into being by Lambeth 1968 and meets every two or three years. The most important of these was the third meeting of the council, known as ACC-3, which took place in 1976 in Trinidad, West Indies, and addressed at length several issues connected with ministry, both that of the whole people of God and that of the ordained. Although the council report confuses "ordained ministry" with "ordained priesthood," it has some good things to say about the need for training priests who will be rooted in the life of the congregations and dioceses. In a section on the diaconate, the report cites with approval Lambeth 1968 and Howe's article, adding:

69

> We do not think that the making of deacons on a wider
> scale than hitherto would cause the laity to feel themselves
> to be released from responsibility to serve as well as to
> worship. We would therefore see the Diaconate conferred
> upon men and women who are deeply committed to
> Christ within the Church, and who are performing a
> caring and serving ministry in the world in the name of
> the Church, or who are carrying out a pastoral ministry
> in the Church.[9]

The council urged that deacons be brought forward by their priests and congregations, and that the fundamental requirements to be met are "God's grace, man's response, and the people's recognition." It also outlined three questions: (1) Should formal theological training be separated from necessary preparation for the diaconate? (2) Should dress and title distinguish deacons from lay persons? (3) Should the close relationship of the deacon with the bishop be strengthened?

In 1984 the sixth meeting of the council, in Badagry, Nigeria, observed that the order of deacons as commonly practiced "had degenerated into little more than an apprenticeship for priesthood." At the same time, however, it held up the ideal of the diaconate as a ministry to the poor, the sick, and the marginal, exercised directly under the bishop.

Lambeth Conference 1988 produced no resolutions on the diaconate. In one of the four section reports, however, "Mission and Ministry," the bishops included a discussion of the distinctive diaconate that summarizes the deacon's role in this way: "to focus or be a sign of the ministry of servanthood in the church and in the world" and "to remind the whole church that the essence of ministry is service." But the role of the deacon also includes interpreting the needs, concerns, and hopes of the world to the church. The bishops also observed that in provinces that do not ordain women to the priesthood deacons are rarely distinctively diaconal. In these places deacons are trained like priests for a ministry like that of priests.[10]

One of the unrecognized issues of Lambeth and the ACC, as official bodies studying the diaconate and issuing opinions at the highest levels of the Anglican Communion, is that no deacons have acted as consultants or written papers on the diaconate for any of

the Lambeth conferences issuing reports and resolutions on deacons. Moreover, no deacons have ever sat as members of the ACC
or been present as observers at any council meetings. A small window opened at Lambeth Conference in 1998. On a tour bus,
informed by Archdeacon Dick Pemble of Chicago that there would
be no deacons serving in Lambeth liturgies, Frank Griswold, the
Presiding Bishop of the Episcopal Church, said: "Get me a deacon!
And I would like that deacon to be a woman." On 29 July 1998,
with Griswold as presider, Marcia Stackhouse of Colorado became
the first Anglican deacon to serve at a Lambeth Eucharist.[11]

Despite these limitations in their gathering of data, and in their
experience of deacons, Lambeth and the ACC have continued to be
guided by the call of John Howe for a distinctive diaconate that
operates in the church as a symbol of humble service. Their reports
and resolutions have also reflected the experience of many
churches that have successfully revived the diaconate during the
last two decades.

## OTHER ANGLICAN CHURCHES

The diaconate in the Anglican Communion has kept up a steady,
if unequal, growth. Anglican deacons, like their Roman Catholic
counterparts, are concentrated mainly in North America, with
smaller groups in England and countries with a British or
European heritage. Ordination of deacons in the Third World has
lagged, despite its increasing number of Christians. Statistics gathered for Lambeth 1998 show some 2,434 deacons in the Anglican
Communion (1,158 men and 1,276 women). The largest number
was in the Episcopal Church: 1,785 (904 men and 881 women);
since that time this number has approached 2,400. Other provinces
with deacons were England about 205, Australia 152, Canada 96,
Southern Africa 77, Aotearoa (Maori) 59, New Zealand 25,
Uganda about 20, Scotland 9, Papua New Guinea 6, and a few in
Central America, Southern Cone (South America), Wales, and the
West Indies.

The revival of the diaconate in the Church of England got off to
a shaky start. Howe's essay and the resolution of Lambeth 1968
produced little initial response. In 1974 a working party of the
Advisory Council for the Church's Ministry (ACCM) advised the
church simply to abolish the diaconate, leaving an ordained min-

istry of bishops and presbyters. (The group wanted to emphasize that "service" is the work of all the faithful.) General Synod ignored the advice but made no move to revive the diaconate. In 1977, in a change of heart, the ACCM suggested three options for the diaconate: its continued use as a short stage of preparation for the priesthood, abolition of the order, or an enlargement of the order to include lay workers, deaconesses, and others.

A more positive response began to appear in the Church of England after 1980. In January 1981 a committee of the Deaconess Community of St. Andrew called an ecumenical consultation on the diaconate, held at the Royal Foundation of St. Katherine in east London, attended by many who would be involved in the working of the issue through General Synod and by others who were to begin an experiment in the diocese of Portsmouth. In October the House of Bishops published *The Deaconess Order and the Diaconate*; this was the first step in the process that culminated in the Synod's giving final approval in July 1985 to the Deacons (Ordination of Women) Measure. Women were admitted as deacons in 1987—though for many women the diaconate was only a potential transition to priesthood—and in 1988 the House of Bishops received a report recommending a restoration of the order for men and women. By the end of 1989, 756 deaconesses had been ordained deacon, and there were a few other men and women deacons. In Portsmouth Bishop Timothy Bavin continued a pioneer program begun by his predecessor, Ronald Gordon, with the ordination in 1985 of seven men. By 1998, after many of the women had been ordained priest, the number of active deacons was 155 (41 men and 114 women).

Bishop Bavin was also the principal author of the 1988 report commissioned by the House of Bishops, *Deacons in the Ministry of the Church*.[12] The report surveyed the history and current scope of the order, proposed a theology of a distinctive diaconate based on the *diakonia* received in baptism, and explored the future of the order. The report saw deacons as servants to the wider community, enablers of the church, and servants within the church. All their activity is focused in the liturgy, where the deacon "symbolizes in his or her movement between the people and the altar the union of the whole worshipping community." It concluded by recommending that the Church of England encourage men and women to serve in a distinctive diaconate. General Synod merely noted the report, however, and the House of Bishops in 1989 refused to bring forward specific proposals "because of a lack of theological consensus and practical evidence."[13]

Deacons in England have their own organization. On 29 November 1988 the inaugural meeting of the Diaconal Association of the Church of England (DACE) was held. Unlike the North American Association for the Diaconate, which gives members the right to elect directors, DACE consists only of licensed persons— deacons and deaconesses, some Church Army workers, and accredited lay workers. The chief voice of the diaconate is that of a scholar and journalist, Sr. Teresa of the Community of St. Andrew, a religious order that has had women deacons (formerly deaconesses) since 1862. She grew up in the Boston area, graduated from Harvard Divinity School, and moved to England, where she became a deaconess, in 1987 deacon, and in 1994 priest. Dressed in her blue habit, and (until 2002, when arthritis reduced her mobility) wearing a helmet and riding a motorcycle, Teresa was a familiar sight and illustrious character in the tough Notting Hill section where the sisters had their motherhouse. In 1981 she organized the ecumenical consultation on the diaconate in London, began the newsletter *Distinctive Diaconate News* and the scholarly series Distinctive Diaconate Studies, and joined the battle that resulted in the ordaining of women deacons. Her newsletter tells everything you want to know about deacons in the Anglican Communion and other churches. In addition to news about England, the British Isles, and far-flung provinces, it contains a calendar of events and deacon saints and lists new books and other publications.[14]

Efforts to restore the diaconate have been undertaken in several other churches of the Anglican Communion. In Canada the General Synod in 1989 "commended" a plan to restore the order. Several dioceses have developed programs, and the number of deacons continues to grow. In the Province of Southern Africa official permission for a diaconate of men and women was granted in 1983, to be handled by each diocese, but the number of deacons remains small. The bishops hoped for deacons to help the families of those in prison, often the victims of apartheid. The Scottish Episcopal Church approved a diaconate for men in 1965—although few men took advantage of the opportunity—and in 1986 opened the order to women. Several other provinces allow women to be deacons but refuse to allow them to be priests.

In Australia a revival of the diaconate has taken place, with strength especially in the metropolitan dioceses of Melbourne, Sydney, and Brisbane. Some dioceses have deacons serving as archdeacons. The Australian Anglican Diaconal Association (AADA), formerly a deaconess fellowship, represents men and women deacons.

The retired New Testament scholar Reginald H. Fuller visited Australia in 1987–88 and found the women deacons "just getting into their stride" in Canberra—but not in the liturgy. His use of a woman deacon in the liturgy created a strong impression, and later in a speech at the diocesan synod he advocated the full liturgical use of deacons. "Unfortunately, my remarks were misunderstood," he later wrote.

> The women deacons present at the Synod thought that I was degrading them by suggesting that they lay the table and wash the dishes! I guess the trouble was that they thought of themselves as transitional deacons who hoped to be advanced to the priesthood. They did not appreciate that it was the dignity of the deacon to serve at table as well as to serve in the world. Unfortunately, I did not have a chance to explain that this was not a job for female deacons only and that a male deacon, properly used, would do the same chore.[15]

In New Zealand the main changes have been attitudinal rather than structural. One of the few male deacons, Peter Sykes, reports that he wanted to become a deacon "so that I could work in the church's name in the community," but as a compromise he first had to train for the priesthood in seminary. Now the church has begun to awaken. In 1988 a report to the General Synod advocated experimentation with a diaconate of "caring, sacrificial service," and today the diaconate is alive and well, especially in Christchurch and Auckland. By 2004 growth had taken place also in Wales, and a bishops' commission in Nigeria had recommended restoration of the order as a permanent vocation.

Some Anglican provinces have stumbled in their attempt to have deacons. In 1986 the diocese of Chile proposed reviving the diaconate as a practical ministry and also proposed ordaining presbyteral candidates directly to the priesthood after a period as a licensed "assistant pastor"—but the province, the Southern Cone of South America, narrowly defeated the motion in synod, largely on the grounds that bishops and priests should never lose sight of their *diakonia*. Once again confusion between the theological virtues of *agape* and *diakonia* led to practical disorder.

Revival of the diaconate in Anglican churches has tended to follow renewal of liturgy. Strangely, only a few of the contemporary eucharistic liturgies provide for the use of deacons. The Anglican churches in the United States and Canada give more rubrical instructions than any others, and hence they make fuller provision for deacons in the liturgy. In most other provinces the liturgies scarcely mention deacons. The Church of England provides alternative services in *Common Worship*, including this general note to the Eucharist:

> In some traditions the ministry of the deacon at Holy
> Communion has included some of the following elements:
> the bringing in of the Book of the Gospels, the invitation
> to confession, the reading of the Gospel, the preaching of
> the sermon when licensed to do so, a part in the prayers
> of intercession, the preparation of the table and the gifts,
> a part in the distribution, the ablutions and the dismissal.

A following sentence states, however, that "an assisting priest, a Reader, or another episcopally authorized minister" may perform the deacon's liturgical ministry. In many other countries a reader proclaims the gospel, the intercessions are led by the president or by the minister or leader, and what happens at the preparation of the gifts and at communion is sketched out vaguely, if at all. In many churches the presider says the dismissal. The rubrics, or lack of rubrics, make it possible for anyone, including deacons, to function in the traditional diaconal roles. As Reginald Fuller discovered in Australia, the problem will be to teach and explain the diaconal tradition throughout the Anglican Communion.[16]

Fortunately, opportunities for churches to symbolize *diakonia* in the liturgy do not depend on detailed instructions. The spirit of the age embraces freedom and adaptation, rather than restraint and prescription, and these liberal traits will open space in the liturgy for deacons who serve in the world. The general intercessions are an example of liturgy that has been opened up to the people. Over

75

✳

the years forms of prayer have become more flexible and therefore more accessible to a variety of leadership and to congregational participation. The monologues typical of earlier Anglican intercession (including the 1928 Book of Common Prayer of the Episcopal Church) have given way to litanies, to open forms alternating with set texts, to multiple options, to seasonal and occasional prayers, and to prayer that is locally composed and even spontaneous. In many churches it is common for lay persons to create or lead the prayers. As deacons appear more and more in the churches, it will seem right for those who work with the poor and needy to take part, especially to lead, in prayer for them.

Revisions of the ordination liturgy also take deacons more seriously. The ordinal of 1550, virtually unchanged except for the revisions of 1662, endured in most Anglican provinces until the 1980s. In ordaining a deacon, the bishop laid on hands but did not pray, declaring instead: "Take thou Authority to execute the Office of a Deacon in the Church of God committed unto thee; In the Name of the Father, and of the Son, and of the Holy Ghost. Amen" (1928 Book of Common Prayer). The rite nowhere mentioned a bestowal of the Holy Spirit on the candidates. Although this imperative formula appears defective, at least as viewed several centuries later, it reflected Cranmer's belief that deacons already were, as Acts 6:3 says, "full of the Spirit and of wisdom." The apostles simply recognized outwardly what God had already created within. In this sense deacons are distinct from bishops and presbyters, who receive the Spirit in a public ceremony, just as Christ bestowed it on his apostles.

By the late twentieth century Anglican churches abandoned the Cranmerian model and theology of ordination, choosing to follow instead the models of the third and fourth centuries. The typical prayer begins with remembrance of Jesus as servant, who humbled himself and became obedient even to death on a cross, and with thanksgiving for God's call of the deacon. Then the bishop, laying on hands, prays, "Send down the Holy Spirit upon your servant N for the office and work of a deacon in your Church" (Church of England) or some similar invocation. In the 1989 prayer book of New Zealand the ordination prayer reveals a lyric trend in liturgical composition. At the laying on of hands the bishop prays, "God of grace, through your Holy Spirit, gentle as a dove, living, burning as fire, empower your servant N for the office and work of a deacon in the Church." At the end the people shout, "Amen! May *they* proclaim the good news, inspire our prayers, and show us Christ, the Servant."[17]

## ECUMENICAL TRENDS

If the ecumenical movement sometimes stumbles over priests and bishops, it strides easily among deacons. Because they are not responsible for the sacramental life of the church, deacons are in no position to cause disorder through defective consecration. Instead, freed from responsibilities for ordination and liturgical presidency, they easily cross communion lines for mutual formation, projects of charity, and social contacts. Whenever hierarchy throws up walls and even closes the gates, deacons find a way through the barrier.

The ecumenical interest in deacons began soon after Vatican II. In 1964 the World Council of Churches held a consultation on "The Ministry of Deacons in the Church." This meeting resulted in the publication of two studies, *The Ministry of Deacons* (1965) and *The Deaconess* (1966).

In what has become the most influential and famous of ecumenical statements, the Faith and Order Commission, meeting in Lima, Peru, drew up *Baptism, Eucharist and Ministry* (1982), commonly called BEM. Section 31 deals "in a tentative way" with the functions of deacons:

> Deacons represent to the Church its calling as servant in the world. By struggling in Christ's name with the myriad needs of societies and persons, deacons exemplify the interdependence of worship and service in the Church's life. They exercise responsibility in the worship of the congregation: for example by reading the scriptures, preaching and leading the people in prayer. They help in the teaching of the congregation. They exercise a ministry of love within the community. They fulfill certain administrative tasks and may be elected to responsibilities for governance.

A commentary on the section mentions a few issues (whether there is a need for deacons, whether they need to be ordained, whether the order should be used as a stepping stone to the priesthood) and sums up:

Today, there is a strong tendency in many churches to
restore the diaconate as an ordained ministry with its own
dignity and meant to be exercised for life. As the churches
move closer together there may be united in this office
ministries now existing in a variety of forms and under a
variety of names.[18]

Some Protestant churches have moved in response to the BEM
document. Many of them already have deacons of various kinds
and names—deacons, deaconesses, diaconal ministers—some
ordained, mostly lay. An ecumenical working party in Scotland in
1989, representing four traditions (Anglican, Methodist,
Reformed, United), found this variety "not a depressing omen of
the difficulty of reaching agreement, but an encouraging sign of the
manifold grace of God given to the churches even in their separation." Their report, titled "Deacons for Scotland?" called for "reten-
tion of a variety of kinds of deacon in the united church in an initial period, leaving the way fully open for the church, after union,
to discover what the office of deacon in the Church of God is to
be."[19]

Interest in the diaconate among Methodists in New Zealand
surfaced in 1984, when David S. Mullan wrote a small but important book, *Diakonia and the Moa*, in which he compared deacons to
the moa, an extinct bird of that country, and urged the revival of
the seemingly perished diaconate. In 1996 the United Methodist
Church in the United States began to ordain deacons as full members of the clergy—and stopped ordaining transitional deacons—
and by 2000 there were more than 1,000 of them. Methodist
deacons, with stole attached under the right arm, serve alongside
diaconal ministers, not ordained, who wear the stole hanging
straight down from the left shoulder.

In the Eastern Orthodox and Oriental churches women deacons
(or deaconesses) are canonically possible, but women are currently
ordained only in the Armenian Apostolic and two other Oriental
churches. According to ancient custom, the wife of a deacon may be
called deaconess. There is a movement in Orthodox theological circles to revive the apostolic order of deaconess on the basis of many
ancient prototypes and prayers. Among several important studies,
Kyriaki Karidoyanes Fitzgerald, a Greek Orthodox theologian, has
reviewed the history and advocated the restoration of deacons.[20]

Lutherans already have thousands of men and women deacons in Europe, some of them (mainly in Sweden) ordained by bishops in apostolic succession. The union of three Lutheran churches into the Evangelical Lutheran Church in America resulted in a moratorium in the ordination of deacons, but pressure for a restored diaconate continued. Following a five-year study, the Churchwide Assembly in 1993 turned down a recommendation for ordained deacons. Instead, the ELCA decided to consecrate diaconal ministers, lay ministers but otherwise barely distinguishable from ordained deacons, vested in dalmatics but not stoles. Many Lutherans have a hard time accepting any ministerial ordering that is not concentrated in the office of pastor (that is, presbyter). As a consequence, the agreement *Called to Common Mission* between the Episcopal Church and the ELCA, in 2000, celebrating full communion between the two churches, gave lukewarm and unsatisfactory treatment to deacons and diaconal ministers, suggesting that they, but not priests and bishops, are in need of further study and reform.[21]

Although Anglican dialogue with Lutherans has dealt only tentatively with deacons, Anglican and Lutheran deacons have already made contact, and extended welcome, on their own informal level. Since 1982 the Episcopal Church has had "interim eucharistic sharing" with the ELCA. On the basis of that communion the board of trustees of NAAD decided in June 1989 to include Lutheran synods (the equivalent of dioceses) and deacons in its membership.

A major ecumenical event occurred in 1996. After two years of preliminary papers, consultations, and drafting, the Anglican-Lutheran International Commission issued the Hanover Report, formally titled *The Diaconate as Ecumenical Opportunity*. The report lays a theological basis, outlines the meaning and function of the ministry, and proposes a restored diaconate in both traditions. One challenge was "the possibility of direct ordination to the priesthood."[22]

In many countries organizations and periodicals exist for each denomination that has deacons or diaconal ministers. In Europe such groups are prominent especially in Germany, France, Italy, and England. National types of the diaconate have evolved, which transcend denominational barriers. In Germany the Roman Catholic and Evangelical deacons tend to administer church charities, and the Evangelical social-care diaconate is slowly evolving into a ministry of word and liturgy like that of the Roman Catholic diaconate. In England the Roman Catholic and Anglican deacons tend to be liturgical and pastoral ministers in parishes, but the revival of the Anglican diaconate has resulted in greater emphasis on social care. Sr. Teresa of London, observing the similarities and cross-culturization in 1989, suggested that it is more possible for deacons than for priests or pastors to work ecumenically in joint projects or with mixed recipients.[23]

The evolving fellowship of deacons is expressed through several international organizations. The largest of these is the World Federation of Diaconal Associations and Sisterhoods, known as Diakonia, founded in 1946. Diakonia began as an organization of mainly protestant and women's associations, heavily Lutheran and Methodist, with some Anglican deaconesses, but its composition has changed to include both men and women's "diaconal communities." Diakonia holds an international assembly every four years, and operates mainly for the exchange of information. A related group, Kaire, founded in 1978, specializes in sharing spiritual insights through annual meetings, and includes Roman Catholics and Orthodox as well as Anglicans and Protestants. Finally, the Roman Catholics have their own worldwide group, Internationales Diakonatszentrum (IDZ), which evolved out of the original diaconate circles in 1959. Located in Rottenburg, Germany, IDZ acts as a clearing house for information and holds seminars and conferences.

In all the ecumenical and international discussions, three themes continually appear: the theology of service and servants in the context of baptism, the spirituality of serving and being served, and identification of the needs of the world and their root causes. The participation of deacons in the ecumenical movement is a late but fitting phenomenon. Diaconal ministry is alive and well. In churches with deacons, ordained or unordained, they serve the local assembly, they serve the poor, they serve the diocese (or equivalent) directly under the bishop (or equivalent), and they serve church unity. In churches without deacons but with other diaconal ministers, or whatever they are called, these persons also serve the assembly, the poor, and the ecumenical church. As all churches enter into dialogue, they discover that they are caring for the same poor and representing the same servant Christ.

CHAPTER SIX

# THE FINDING, NURTURE, AND CARE OF DEACONS

Good deacons are found, not made, but once found they must be cultivated. Tend them, touch them, lay hands on them with prayer. Like any new plant in the garden, they need fertilizer and water, protection from bugs and disease, potting, propping, and pruning, space to grow, and most of all words of encouragement. With these as our general principles, this chapter will deal with the particulars: diaconate programs, selection, preparation for ordination, and the life and work of deacons. Let us look at the realities and the rules.



## DIACONATE PROGRAMS

Since the mid-1970s diaconate programs have spread and developed in the Episcopal Church. Like any human endeavor, they are subject to the will, imagination, and skills of those who create and sustain them. Some programs are weak and dispirited, some clericalized, some constrained by fear and control. Many programs, though, are highly organized and effective, dedicated to the mission of the church, and led by deacons with administrative and teaching skills.

Since 1997 annual meetings of archdeacons and other program directors have enabled them to share insights, borrow from each other, and develop common approaches. One fruit of these meeting has been national guidelines, used by dioceses as a basis for their own guidelines.

Experience over many years teaches that three conditions must exist for a program to be healthy, energetic, and beneficial:

First, the bishop should hold a clear theology of the diaconate as a full and equal order, grounded in scriptural and patristic concepts of *agape*-filled *diakonia,* or sending forth on sacred missions, and coherent with the theology expressed in the catechism and ordination rite. The bishop should understand the theology and teach it to the priests and people of the diocese. It is important that the priests and key lay persons support the bishop in carrying out a diaconate program.

Second, the diocese should be committed to the program in terms of people, time, and money. Directing the program should be the major responsibility of one person or the substantial responsibility of several, and those in charge should plan ahead for at least several years. How this works depends on the diocese's size, geography, demographics, and financial resources. Small or poor dioceses are just as able to commit people, time, and money as large or rich ones. They just don't commit them in the same way or in the same quantities.

Third, deacons should be in charge. A council on deacons, consisting of deacons, priests, and lay persons, is needed to oversee the program. The council assists the bishop, standing committee, and commission on ministry in selection and formation, and it plans and carries out the collegial life and work of the deacons. As a program matures, the bishop should appoint a deacon as archdeacon. Accountable to the bishop, the archdeacon functions as director of the program, works with the bishop and the commission on ministry to administer the program, and may chair the council on deacons. The director of formation should be a separate person with experience in adult education; preferably a deacon, the director may also have the title of archdeacon.

Governing the ordination and ministry of deacons are two major parts of the Title III canons on ministry: Canon 6 (Of the Ordination of Deacons) and Canon 7 (Of the Life and Work of Deacons), enacted by General Convention in 2003.[1] These canons contain everything necessary for ordaining and regulating the deacons of a diocese, without the need to refer to any other canon. They fit together, one after the other, so that the diaconate can be seen and treated as a unified order. Canonical steps, interviews, documents, and other procedures are greatly simplified, reduced to less than one-third of those in earlier canons. More important, these canons reflect a major thematic shift from diaconate as individual aspiration, concerning those who apply, study, and minister often unaccompanied by others, to diaconate as community, concerning those chosen by others, nurtured by and among others, and serving with and among others. Reflecting the Seven of Acts 6, deacons are selected by a local community of faith from those in their midst, formed with others for mission and ministry, and incorporated into a diocesan community of deacons, closely related in special ways to the bishop and all others who minister. They are ordained for the mission of the church, serving under the bishop, serving all people.

The canons also reflect a growing understanding about the theological locus of the diaconate. Deacons serve the church as messengers, agents, and attendants (roles close to the probable original meaning of *diakonos* as one who acts as an agent or go-between). They are signs of Christ's own eternal role as *diakonos* or agent of God in creation and salvation. As messengers they proclaim the good news to the poor. As agents they represent the needs of the world to the church and call the body of Christ to the work of transforming the world by striving "for justice and peace among all people." As attendants they stand at the altar week after week as the faithful gather to "continue in the apostles' teaching and fellowship, in the breaking of bread, and in the prayers."

## SELECTION

> The Bishop, in consultation with the Commission, shall establish procedures to identify and select persons with evident gifts and fitness for ordination to the Diaconate. [Canon III.6.1]

The canon provides for a congregation to "nominate" a person for ordination to the diaconate. The only prerequisite is that the person must be a "confirmed adult communicant in good standing." The nomination must be in writing and include a "letter of support" signed by the priest and at least two-thirds of the vestry. No longer does someone apply for the diaconate.

Actually, priests have been identifying and putting forward "persons with evident gifts and fitness" for centuries, and more recently ordinary Christians have contributed to the process. What is new is the change in emphasis. Formerly deacons were thought of as receiving an inner call from the Holy Spirit, and the church responded with assent and validation. Now they receive an outer call from the church, and those who are inwardly disposed to the ministry of deacon are moved to accept. The old canons on ministry reflected a theology of personal inspiration to vocation, while the new see the bestowal of holy orders as a function of the body of Christ. God the Holy Spirit calls through the church. This theology, although scriptural and ancient, had almost vanished before the reforms of the late twentieth century. In ordination rites today the bishop asks: Are you "truly called by God and his Church?" in contrast to the older version: Are you "inwardly moved by the Holy Ghost?"

The importance of an inner call has not vanished, however; it reveals itself in service in the community, good reputation, and willingness to act as deacon. But the outer call claims first place; it also comes from God, but it is spoken within the church. No longer are we to wait for applicants who have been inwardly moved before we test and screen and validate them; instead we are to recruit those with gifts of diaconal ministry, select those who are qualified, and call them.

How this is supposed to work is not as clear as the principle. Cast lots? Elect? Some subtler mechanism? An action of the entire congregation? Of the priest and vestry alone? Without saying how, the canon leaves the specifics to the bishop, who consults with the commission on ministry. Selection of deacons occurs as part of a larger process whereby the church discerns the needs of the church's own life and of the world and the gifts of the church's people. Dioceses and congregations first help all people to discover and evaluate their own ministries. When this has been done, each local church, each congregation, can identify and raise up priests, deacons, and various other ministries from its own membership.

Persons considered for the diaconate should normally have undergone discernment in community (as set forth in Canon III.3), so that they will be equipped to respond to the nomination and to enter the ordination process. As a consequence of discernment, the community learns to distinguish between those suited for priesthood and those suited for diaconate. Priests gather a congregation, sustain it, and give it a vision of God's mission. Hence they need skills in formation, organization, and administration, in presiding in the liturgy, and in preaching the gospel. Deacons start, encourage, and sustain the ministry of other baptized persons in the world. Hence they need skills in helping people, mediation, and advocacy, in leading teams of ministers, and in performing a liturgical role as angels, messengers, and agents. When Christians show the community that they are priestly or diaconal, the community can call them as priests or deacons.

The initial stage of selection is a delicate period in which the congregation plays a crucial role. It must also be willing to involve itself in the preparation of persons for the diaconate. The parish that has never seen a deacon must find out more about them by inviting deacons to speak and perform in the liturgy. Obviously the parish where deacons are to officiate must clearly want them, as must the priest. After that, the congregation must be carefully prepared, potential deacons screened, and a thoughtful consensus reached. Finally, the potential deacons may or may not have considered the diaconate before their nomination. They have the right to accept or to refuse this call.

The personal qualifications of a potential deacon are drawn from Acts 6:3 and 1 Timothy 3:8–13. Men and women chosen for the diaconate should be "of good standing, full of the Spirit and of wisdom." If they are loyal and committed to family, community, and church, they have good standing in the eyes of their fellow Christians. If they are disciple-formed, gospel-centered, and mission-driven, they are full of the Spirit. If they passionately find Christ in the hungry, thirsty, stranger, naked, sick, and imprisoned, lead Christian people in loving care of the poor, sick, lonely, and needy, and defend those who have no helper, they are full of wisdom. They "hold fast to the mystery of the faith with a clear conscience." They have the heart of a deacon.

We can trust God to act through the gathered people. Acts 6 suggests a process begun and completed entirely within a community of believers, and quickly. The local Christian people select or elect—the precise method depends on circumstances—from among those with good qualifications. From such persons each congregation chooses one or two deacons (maybe more, if the congregation is large). The decision to ordain, made by the bishop, comes near the beginning of the process, soon after the congregation has nominated. The church says yes at the beginning and sticks with it while the person prepares for ordination.

Ordination is a process, in which each step is part of a spiritual journey, a passage to a new role in the Christian community. Thus the canon on ordination makes a sharp distinction between selection (nomination and postulancy) and preparation (candidacy). Once selection has taken place—that is, when the bishop has admitted a person to candidacy—preparation for ordination begins, and it continues without any major gates, barriers, or hoops to jump through. Because deacons serve in close relationship to the bishop, the bishop is clearly seen as the chief person who selects them, determines their preparation, and oversees their ministry. The bishop does so not alone, of course, but with advice and help from others.

When a congregation has nominated someone for the diaconate, the bishop may admit him or her as a postulant. Originally, postulancy was a period of probation and testing, and the canon restores it to that purpose. Postulancy is "a process of exploration of and decision on the Postulant's call to the diaconate." Following "a thorough investigation of the Postulant" and an interview by the bishop or someone else, the commission on ministry or "a designated committee" interviews the person and makes a recommendation. The usual background checks and medical and psychological exams come early in the process, so that the bishop and commission will have full information in hand for the interviews and final decision. The bishop then decides whether to admit the person as a candidate.

As a candidate, the person begins preparing for ordination. Although the length of formation is not specified, and each bishop will determine an appropriate period, candidacy must last at least a year. The bishop may leave the candidate in the same congregation to emphasize the localness of ministry, or may move the candidate elsewhere, at least for several months, to give a broader experience.

## PREPARATION FOR ORDINATION

Getting ready for ordination is only a small part of a lifelong process. Formation begins in the womb, includes the grace received in baptism, and continues for life and even beyond the grave. Canon law uses the term *preparation* to refer to the course of study and training for ordination. Preparation for ordination involves a specific application of formation, in which a person learns the rudiments of how to function in the symbolic role of deacon.

Preparation takes place in community and involves formation in five general areas in which candidates must "demonstrate basic competence." Formation in each area should be designed to enhance the distinct nature of deacons as Christian persons, attached to the bishop, who have a special responsibility for leading the church in *caritas* (charity) and *justicia* (justice).

Here are some ways to flesh out the five general areas:

### 1. Academic studies

Thorough knowledge of the Bible comes first, followed closely by immersion in the tradition of the church. Through study and discussion, candidates can acquire a basic knowledge of the church's doctrine, liturgy, history, ethics and moral theology, and spiritual tradition. Using such knowledge, they should be able to identify ancient heresies in today's church and to reflect theologically on contemporary concerns.

### 2. Diakonia and the diaconate

Meanings of *diakonia* and *diakonos* have evolved during the history of the church. Forces shaping their definitions include the biblical and primitive roots of the diaconate, drastic changes in ministerial order and practice in the medieval and modern churches, and the contemporary commitment of deacons to mercy and justice.

### 3. Human awareness and understanding

A new area in diaconal formation, human awareness includes developing the capacity to relate to others in healthy ways. Candidates should enter into dialogue with those who differ (including different interpretations of theology and scripture), articulating biases in race, sex, culture, and class, and dealing with people of diverse ages and generations. Training in sexual conduct, Title IV (canons on discipline), and anti-racism, all required by the canon, also belongs in this area.

### 4. Spiritual development and discipline

Spiritual observances commonly required include the Sunday Eucharist and daily office, daily meditation and other forms of prayer, and daily reading of the Bible. Candidates need to develop commitment, accountability, and obedience. By using resources such as a spiritual director and retreats, and by learning to share the love of Christ through evangelical and charitable contacts, they deepen their spiritual being.

### 5. Practical training and experience

A key piece of practical formation is supervised practice in pastoral ministries of care or other specialties. Often such training takes the form of Clinical Pastoral Education (CPE) or the equivalent, depending on the availability of courses. Candidates should also have practice in collaborative leadership and in the deacon's role in liturgy. Much training can be accomplished through field work in other congregations and ministry sites.

Dioceses are expected to adapt formation to the local culture and to the gifts and needs of each candidate. Many candidates may already have been in formation for the diaconate, both in formal settings and in life experience, which should be taken into account. Not everyone should prepare for ordination in the same way. While candidates prepare as a group, the program of preparation should fit the needs of each candidate. The diaconate is a polychrome ministry with a great diversity of types, and ideally programs will help people prepare in ways suitable to each individual and each proposed ministry. The oldest type of diaconate training in the Episcopal Church was reading for orders: private study under the direction of one or more tutors. Because solitary study does a poor job of preparing a person for communal ministry, this type has all but vanished. Even in remote settings, or in dioceses with no other candidates, other Christians can be included in formation. Many dioceses find it desirable to train deacons in small groups, where candidates reflect on and share what they have read and practiced. They learn to think theologically about their ministries of social care, and to deal emotionally and spiritually with pain, disappointment, and failure. It is sometimes helpful for such groups to include spouses.

Three main types of preparation have emerged in the Episcopal Church: the diocesan school for deacons, the diocesan school of theology or ministry, or some combination of the two.

The diocesan school for deacons focuses on training for the diaconate, and is highly successful at building a community of deacons; it provides role models, creates diaconal identity, and involves the sharing of stories. Early schools were organized along seminary lines; one school had state certification and even awarded degrees (e.g., bachelor of the diaconate). The tendency, reflected in the canon, is to emphasize a more practical and experiential range of formation.

The diocesan school of theology or ministry prepares an assortment of persons: those not seeking ordination at all, candidates for the diaconate, and in some dioceses, candidates for the priesthood. In some dioceses this type of school makes use of programs like the four-year curriculum "Education for Ministry" (EFM) for the academic portion. In many places EFM *is* the school for ministry, with groups meeting once a week during the academic year for four years in many scattered locations. Written materials cover the history of the people of God from the sources of the Pentateuch to the present day.

The length of preparation for ordination to the diaconate normally ranges from two to four years. An overly extended period deprives parishes and dioceses of the deacons they have selected, while deacons requiring more than four years to complete formation should probably be dropped from the program. If the person is already diaconal, lengthy preparation is unnecessary. The seven men of Acts 6 were already formed in the way of Christ, although the apostles laid hands on them with what some today might call undue haste. Similarly, in the modern church preparation for ordination can be short and concentrated. Since theological knowledge is no longer the privilege and sole possession of bishops and presbyters, many "ordinary" Christians are thoroughly familiar with the Bible, discuss theology and ethics in depth, and possess skills for ministry. If we choose diaconal Christians, they will already have many skills needed for the diaconate.

Evaluations and assessments help the bishop and others determine whether the candidate is ready to be ordained. There is movement away from the academic style of written and oral examinations, and toward a form of evaluation in which the candidate participates actively, and which provides guidance for continuing education. The role of the Standing Committee is clearly defined as certifying the legality of the process and the absence of a "sufficient objection."

Increasingly, deacons are ordained as a class, on some special occasion or during diocesan convention. Individual deacons are sometimes ordained in the congregation that nominated them, and to which they will be assigned. In some dioceses the bishop uses the ordination liturgy to celebrate the ministries of all the people, of whom one or a few happen to be deacons.[2]

Finally, I wish to set forth a statement of priorities. In the process of ordaining a deacon, all the parts have value. If we select "diaconal people," the diaconate will follow. Preparation is important chiefly for developing a spirit of community. For deacons the most enduring part of their formation takes place after ordination, lasts for life, and takes account of changing circumstances in the life and ministry of the deacons.

## THE LIFE AND WORK OF DEACONS

Canon 7 emphasizes the collegiality of the diaconate, as a "Community of Deacons" with a special relationship with the bishop. Individually and as a collegial body, deacons carry out the bishop's will as they serve all people and especially the poor, sick, weak, and oppressed. The deacon's ministry is thus linked with the bishop's own duty to show mercy and compassion and "to defend those who have no helper."[3] The bishop may appoint one or more archdeacons (some dioceses have more than one, with regional or functional jurisdictions) and a "Council on Deacons" to administer the diaconate program. At the first writing of this book in 1991 there were four such archdeacons; at the second writing in 2004 there are forty-three.

The bishop may assign deacons to congregations or to "non-parochial ministries," increasing the options for ministry in church and world. Although most deacons should have a congregational base, the bishop may wish to place a deacon on special assignment. Since the role of deacons does not normally include presiding,[4] the canon allows deacons to be "administrators" of congregations but prohibits them from being in charge.

Deacons who serve mainly on a congregational staff—although much of their work may be outside the church—are commonly known as parish deacons. They serve under the oversight of the bishop, in collaboration with the priest (who has authority in all matters concerning the congregation), working with the people to develop ministries in the world. This is the most common type of deacon.

Deacons who serve mainly on the diocesan staff are commonly known as diocesan deacons. They serve under the immediate oversight of the bishop or of someone appointed by the bishop. Normally these deacons are also assigned to a congregation, sometimes the cathedral, where they serve in the liturgy and may have other parish functions. Diocesan deacons, especially those appointed archdeacon, help to strengthen the relationship between bishop and diocese. Within the diocesan family, they provide diaconal ministries of administration, oversight, and education.

Deacons who serve for the most part outside the church are sometimes known as professional (or special) deacons, although they share many similarities with both parish-based and diocese-based deacons. They too are assigned to a congregation as their liturgical base, but their external occupation is usually professional and salaried, involving employment at state or private institutions, where they minister in hospitals, prisons, social agencies, and similar establishments. In this role they help congregations relate more effectively to the government or public sector. This professional category also includes deacons who are members of religious orders; despite potential conflict between vows of obedience to a bishop and to a religious superior, several orders have called members to the diaconate.

Sending deacons into fields of ministry is part of the mission of the church, the bishop's ancient and vital function of assigning deacons to work in the church and the world. In many dioceses the bishop assigns deacons to the congregation that nominated them, or to the cathedral or some other congregation, after consultation with the priest. There they function under the surrogate leadership and authority of the priest. It is important to understand that deacons in congregations are not "curates" or "assistants" selected at the priest's discretion. They are "deacons," often called by the congregation out of its membership, and appointed by the bishop as the bishop's deputies and emissaries.

In some dioceses the bishop appoints deacons to another congregation than the one from which they came, or rotates deacons every few years. This practice is feasible in compact or metropolitan dioceses. Elsewhere it may cause hardship for the deacons and their families. In every diocese, deacons must be ready and able to respond to the bishop's call to minister anywhere in the diocese. Flexibility and adaptability—the characteristics of Stephen and Philip—sometimes call for change of place or ministry or both. Some bishops leave deacons in the same place and same ministry until old age or death, while others move them often, but such policies do not always take into account the needs of the person or of the community. The support of the priest and congregation should be a continuing requirement, periodically renewed. But the deacon's personality, family, job, talents, and changing circumstances are equally important. The deacon too has a right to be consulted and to request or consent to assignment, including a change.

Most parish deacons serve the church part time without cash stipend, housing, or housing allowance, although some are paid a stipend. The congregation may, and probably should, cover expenses such as a car allowance and funds for continuing education. The diocese may provide for deacons to participate in the group life insurance and medical insurance programs of the diocese, usually at their own expense.

Diocesan and professional deacons are usually assigned to the cathedral or to the congregation from which they were originally called. Diocesan deacons function in a variety of jobs: administrators, archdeacons, chancellors, treasurers, secretaries, business managers, office staff, directors of religious education, journalists, and holders of other professional positions. They may also be institutional workers such as chaplains, social workers, and agency directors. Professional deacons perform in many of the same jobs, but outside the church.

Important diocesan positions are held by many deacons. In several dioceses a deacon works as director of the diocesan camp or conference center, while it is increasingly common for deacons to provide assistance to the church, with a strong element of outreach, on the level of a parish, deanery, region, or ecumenical group.

Although ordination to the diaconate permanently confers the grace to symbolize Christ the *diakonos* and his diaconal church, assignments are not always permanent. Deacons who move to another community or diocese, or who cease to function in a congregation or diocese, lose the right to function as deacon and to symbolize *diakonia*, unless they receive a new assignment. Deacons who arrive in a new congregation may not function as deacon until assignment by the bishop, after consultation with the priest.

Once assigned, deacons function in three primary areas: pastoral care among the church's own people, social care in society at large, and liturgy. Christ's washing of his disciples' feet in John 13:1–15 symbolizes the divine love needed in all three areas. In the congregation deacons help by organizing teams to visit the sick, infirm, and newcomers, by leading music, teaching children or adults (especially in the preparation of catechumens), organizing retreats and other spiritual activities, training readers and acolytes, leading prayer and discussion groups, editing and writing for newspapers and newsletters, and working in parish or diocesan administration. These deacons support the baptized in their ministries in the wider community.

In the area of social outreach, deacons lead and encourage others in works of mercy and justice outside the church with prisoners, the old, the sick, the poor, the homeless, the handicapped, abused women, alcoholics, addicts, and their families, and numerous others in need. They also discern this calling in others and encourage them in their vocation. Deacons are involved in politics, business, culture, and local community development. Some social ministries unfold as part of the professional occupation of deacons, and not only with the obvious examples of deacon doctors, nurses, lawyers, and teachers. The church may also decide to put some deacons on salary to perform a vital social ministry.

In the liturgy, deacons visibly enact the *diakonia* of Christ and his church in the Eucharist. Representing both angelic messenger and ordinary table waiter, deacons proclaim the gospel, lead the prayers of the people, wait on the table, administer the cup, dismiss the people, give directions, and keep order. On the three days of the paschal feast (Maundy Thursday night, Good Friday, and the Easter Vigil), deacons play a major role in enacting the mystery of Christ's death and resurrection. Deacons also organize ministries of communion—taking the eucharistic bread and wine to the sick and infirm and directing the eucharistic ministers and eucharistic visitors—and they assist in Christian initiation, marriage, and burial. In liturgies with the bishop it is proper for three or more deacons to serve, and one or two deacons are appropriate in the typical parish liturgy.[5]

93

In a few limited situations, deacons are permitted to preside. This permission is to be considered an aberration, since deacons symbolize diaconal ministry best when they act as messengers and attendants. Deacons may preside, however, at a communion service (this term is preferable to "deacon's mass") or liturgy including distribution of the reserved sacrament to a congregation. This is a liturgy that should be used only when no priest is available and the permission of the bishop has been received either in advance or soon after (in an emergency). Both deacons and lay persons may also anoint the sick when necessary, using oil previously blessed by a bishop or priest; they may *hear* confessions of sin, but they may not pronounce absolution. In all liturgies and sacramental rites the normal presider is a bishop or priest.

Another area of confusion with the priestly role is preaching. Only bishops and priests are ordained specifically to preach. At ordination the bishop directs a candidate for priest to preach, but gives no such direction to a candidate for deacon, who is told instead "to interpret." The bishop may license baptized persons to preach liturgical homilies, after study and practice, but there is no canonical provision for licensing deacons. Some bishops assume that deacons automatically have the ability or right to preach as an extension of the bishop's ministry. Some bishops grant licenses to deacons. Those who are talented preachers may be given appropriate opportunities to exercise this gift.

Sometimes deacons ignore or break the ordination mandate to serve the helpless. Diaconal ministry not only refers to a parish assignment; it includes works of mercy and justice in the world. Failure to incorporate good works constitutes a firm ground for withdrawing an assignment to function liturgically.

Although the deacons of the ancient church were often the chief aides of their bishops, in the modern church many deacons seldom get to see or talk with their bishop. Deacons should seek out special occasions to be with the bishop, not only in the liturgy, but also in settings that foster mutual knowledge and understanding. In small dioceses the bishop can sit down once a year with each deacon to evaluate performance, share opinions, isolate areas of conflict, and set goals. In larger dioceses the task often falls to the archdeacon.

Many bishops clear their schedule to attend meetings and retreats of the community of deacons. In several dioceses the deacons write down brief accounts of their ministry. Their stories are collected, shared among the deacons at the meeting, and delivered to the bishop. In some places the deacons write the bishop an annual letter, like the Ember Week letters of candidates.

But not all is well. It may happen that a bishop who is supportive of deacons retires and is replaced by a bishop who is not. Some bishops want to support their deacons but are confused about their meaning and functions. Some frequently change their minds. Some are fuzzy about resolving conflicts. Some dioceses lose track of their deacons completely, while others never bother to ask. A contact person in one diocese with a large number of deacons reported, "No one at the diocesan house knows what the deacons are doing!" Deacons who should be the bishop's eyes and ears have been allowed to slip into the shadows and become invisible. Partly this is the fault of deacons who forget their ordination vow to "be guided by the pastoral direction and leadership" of the bishop, but the main responsibility belongs to the bishop who swore to "guide and strengthen the deacons."

Parish deacons should consult frequently with the priest in order to monitor their effectiveness, review assignments, and evaluate spiritual and professional growth. Just as deacons have a voice (and usually a vote) in diocesan convention, they need to have a voice in the vestry. The congregation has the right to hear their voice, and the deacons have the duty to speak.

Deacons who work mainly outside the institutional church sometimes come into conflict with their priest, who may expect them to help within the congregation. At the outset of the assignment, there needs to be clarity about the deacon's role, and periodically thereafter a review of expectations and changing circumstances.

In the congregation, areas of conflict may occur in the liturgy, where deacons and other baptized persons have been granted overlapping roles. Although deacons normally lead the prayers of the people and administer the sacrament, they should include others in functions the church finds useful or meaningful, allowing others to participate in leadership. Deacons do not normally function in liturgical roles proper to priests or other persons. Similarly priests do not normally vest as a deacon or act as a deacon in the liturgy (although in the absence of a deacon they may perform diaconal functions).[6]

With so many possibilities for stumbling, deacons need to be members of support groups on several levels: with lay persons, including spouse and family, both in and outside the parish; with other deacons, informally with spouses and formally in meetings; and with presbyters, both socially and formally with the priests of an area, including meetings of the local clericus (clergy of a deanery or convocation).

Canon 7 permits letters of agreement and requires annual reports, both of which are common. In the letter a congregation should clearly set forth the terms involved in a deacon's work, including areas of responsibility, hours of work, annual vacation, sabbatical, and reimbursement of expenses. Although there is no absolute standard for such terms, which vary from place to place, parish-based deacons who are otherwise employed commonly work for the church ten or more hours a week without financial remuneration. Sabbatical leave for study, research, and reflection is usually granted at the rate of three to six months every seven years.

The canon requires continuing education for both priests and deacons. Dioceses should develop a list of resources—including local and online programs—as well as sponsor their own programs. The five general areas of preparation (in Canon 6 above) provide a framework for lifelong formation. Dioceses should require deacons to record continuing education in their annual reports.

Although the canon permits deacons to be administrators of congregations, it makes a sharp distinction between an administrative role and a presiding role. Deacons may be chaplains in institutions, a role in which many deacons already serve, some with professional certification.

The canon also provides for licensing or transferring deacons who move into another diocese, and for retirement. A deacon who wishes to minister as a deacon in the new diocese must, after two months, either get a license from the bishop or transfer into the diocese. The transfer provision is parallel to that for priests. There is no specified age for retirement, which occurs with the consent or at the request of the bishop; the bishop may assign retired deacons for a year at a time. The reasons for retirement are "age or infirmity," categories subject to wide latitude. For each deacon, the bishop should make decisions about retirement in consultation with the deacon, archdeacon, and others as needed.

The finding, nurture, and care of deacons, then, is a community enterprise. It includes the bishop, who has sworn to guide and strengthen the deacons and all others who minister in the church, and who has a Christian duty to pay them close attention and stir up their ministry. It includes the presbyters, who build up and lead the church in every place and work with deacons and others in a team that supports ministry. Most important, it includes vast numbers of Christians who, with the deacons, carry out the great work of mercy, justice, and peace among the poor of the Lord.

✳

## CHAPTER SEVEN

# THE ORDINATION OF DEACONS

The orders of the church—bishops, presbyters, and deacons—are ancient, God-given, and good. In a phrase
dating from 1550, the preface to the ordination rites states
that "different ministries," including the three orders, have existed
in the church "from the apostles' time." The three orders came into
being gradually, with local variations, perhaps within the first generation of Christians, certainly within the first century, as "a gift
from God for the nurture of his people and the proclamation of his
Gospel everywhere" (BCP, 510). Because they occur within the
body of Christ, in a communal designation and blessing of certain
members for certain roles, they are sacred. They convey precise
meanings and have significances that other ministries of value,
ancient or modern, do not impart.

The three orders exist within the *laos* or people of God. Some
Episcopalians misinterpret the Catechism where it refers to the
"laity" (which, in the regrettable contemporary sense of the word,
means unordained Christians) as one "ministry" and even implies
that the "laity" are a fourth order. The whole *laos* are thousands of
ministries. Some ministries are symbolic, and some are functional.
Some are the ordinary share of the Christian life. They occur when
Christians believe in God, share with each other, turn from evil,
proclaim the gospel, serve the needy, and seek justice and peace—
any or all of these and more. Some ministries take place in families,
and some at work. Some are specialized, and some are recognized.
Most simply happen in a quiet way. Some are ordained.

In modern writings about holy orders, it is common to see the
terms *sacrament, sign, symbol, mystery,* and *icon.* Despite subtle differences, I hold these terms to have basically the same meaning,

and I use them interchangeably. Speaking of ordained persons as sign, symbol, or mystery has a long history, going back to Ignatius of Antioch. Today the Catechism says that each order "represents" a particular mode of Christ and his church, a term that emphasizes the *anamnesis* or "Christ-recalling" aspect of orders. We may also say that each order is a "sacrament" or "sign," meaning that, in the language of sacramental theology, it is "an outward and visible sign of an inward and spiritual grace," which is Christ in his church. Or that the order is a "symbol" that points to and contains a particular mode of Christ. Or that the order is a "mystery," in the common definition of that term, a profundity beyond human understanding that somehow reveals the death and resurrection of Christ (the paschal mystery). Or that the order is an "icon," or image-window, through which we commune with a particular face of Christ in heaven. In all these terms Christ is the point of reference.

All symbols, by whatever name, are metaphorical. They involve an image or sign that stands for something, and they consist of two elements called (in the science of semiotics) the signifier and the signified or (in sacramental theology) the outward and visible sign and the inward and spiritual grace. The two elements embrace each other, the visible entwining with the invisible. This is why eucharistic bread should be robust and tasty and not wan wafers no reputable baker would produce from the oven. So too with ordained ministers.

Orders of ministry are no mere states of being, to be gazed upon but not handled. Just as marriage is not a onetime sacramental event in the past (the "wedding") but a living sign of the union between Christ and his church, order is not the "ordination" but a living sign of a manner or mode of Christian life and leadership.

What distinguishes those in holy orders from other members of the laos is the power to embody sign language, and the grace to embody it with God's help. They symbolize and incorporate in particular ways various modes of Christ and the numerous ministries belonging in a general way to all the people of God. This happens by a gift of the Spirit. The gift in ordination differs from the gift in baptism. In baptism the Spirit seals a neophyte as a member of the body of Christ; in ordination the Spirit bestows symbolism on one of the members. The gift of orders does not merely bestow a personal or inner change of character; it also extends and adorns the speech of the community. It is song for the speechless, dance for the lame. The Spirit helps the ordained person act out for the assembly the sign language the church has authorized. But the sign works differently for bishops, presbyters, and deacons.

If I were to pick a symbol for bishops, it would be the circle. Bishops encircle the church. A circle protects and preserves what is within; it keeps the shape and the body. The bishops are hands encircling the diocese and the whole church, embracing and incorporating all the faithful. They are also the center of the circle, around whom all gather in faith and order. Some bishops regard their main activity as adventure, risk, and challenge—hands pushing away and out into the world—but the sign language of episcopacy points mainly to catholicity and orthodoxy. The liturgy of ordination talks about the bishop as primarily "called to guard the faith, unity, and discipline of the Church," while the ordination prayer speaks of the bishop as a shepherd and high priest who serves, pardons, offers, and oversees. The role of the bishop is not static but dynamic, for the gospel requires constant reinterpretation in the world at hand.[1]

Presbyters or priests (even to give both titles reveals the ancient confusion surrounding the order) resemble bishops on a local scale. What bishops are to the diocese, presbyters are to the local church. (The term *local church*, as currently used, can refer to both diocese and congregation.) They lead the baptismal and eucharistic life in parishes, join with other presbyters in a college of elders, and share in the bishop's oversight of the diocese. Can we give them a geometric figure? It could be another circle, or circles within the bishop circle, but let us try the vertical line. As priests they symbolize hands uplifted in prayer. Especially in this post-Constantinian church in which our high priestly bishops must usually be someplace else, priests express the royal priesthood of Christ that all enter at baptism.[2]

In a tradition dating from Ignatius of Antioch, deacons are images of Christ the *diakonos* who acts for God the Father. Although the practice of the diaconate has changed drastically through the centuries, the image has remained firm and constant. As helpers and coworkers of the bishop, deacons carry out the mercy and justice and reveal the *diakonia* of Christ and his church, bringing into focus the great variety found in Christian ministry. In a collegial dimension, deacons form a community within the diocese. In a communal dimension, deacons bring their sign of ministry into the *koinonia* of the church. Through activity, word, and example, deacons encourage, enable, enlist, engage, entice, model, lead, animate, stimulate, inspire, inform, educate, permit, organize, equip, empower, and support Christian people in ministry in the world, and they point to the presence of Christ in God's poor. They are signs of service who uncover and explain signs of service. The human dimension of diaconal symbolism suggests that their geometric figure is the horizontal line, the sign of connection, hands reaching hands.

As images of Christ, deacons are images of his church. Other ordained persons and indeed all Christians also represent Christ and his church (as the Catechism says), in various ways, but the typology of deacons has a special focus or symbolism, separate from all the other representations. Deacons are to be life-bearing persons, modest and humble, strong and constant (as the bishop prays in the ordination liturgy), but also swift and active, respected leaders of the church, and, perhaps surprisingly, thorns in the side of the faithful. Thus the symbol has life and vitality. Alongside these personal qualifications, the church has a duty not to conceal or muddy the symbol but to hold it up and make it visible and clear, so that the special iconography of deacons, Christ as *diakonos* of God, will be acted out and portrayed in our midst for the well-being of the body.[3]

One way to study the diaconate is to examine the liturgy of ordination. Here I use the Book of Common Prayer of the Episcopal Church, with two cautions: First, although the prayer book permits more than one ordinand, it assumes only one. Since many dioceses ordain groups of deacons, I have changed all references to plural. Second, the 1985 rite of the Anglican Church of Canada is almost identical to the 1979 rite of the Episcopal Church, with minor differences in order and text, and the rites of other Anglican churches agree in theology and practice.

The liturgy begins with the presentation of ordinands who have been legally "selected." The ordinands must declare the scriptures "to be the Word of God, and to contain all things necessary to salvation," and must swear loyalty and conformity "to the doctrine, discipline, and worship" of the Episcopal Church. The people consent to the ordination and promise to uphold the person in this ministry. After the singing of the ordination or other litany (all kneeling, although in some dioceses the ordinands lie prostrate) and the collect, all sit for the readings.

The readings present some of the scriptural themes meaningful to the diaconate, especially those of proclamation and personal service. For the first reading, either Jeremiah 1:4–10 (the call of Jeremiah) or Ecclesiasticus (Sirach) 39:1–8 (the scribe who studies the scriptures) may be used. Of these, Jeremiah is especially appropriate. Dealing with putting words in the prophet's mouth, the passage is related to the deacon's proclamation of the gospel. Deacons function as primary evangelists in their congregations.

The prayer book gives three choices for the second reading: 2 Corinthians 4:1–6 (which refers to "seeing the light of the gospel of the glory of Christ" and to "ourselves as your slaves for Jesus' sake"), 1 Timothy 3:8–13 (which lists the qualifications of deacons and "the women"), and Acts 6:2–7 (choice of the Seven, traditionally identified as the first deacons). There are two choices for the gospel: Luke 12:35–38 (slaves with "lamps lit" wait for their master to return from the wedding banquet) and Luke 22:24–27 ("I am among you as one who serves"). Although talk about deacons as "slaves" may not be what the congregation should hear, at least the allusion to light and lamps suggests the role of deacons in the Easter Vigil.

The preacher then delivers a homily illuminating the readings and the occasion. There is a custom, whose origin and age I am unable to determine (the prayer book does not mention it), that the preacher close with a "charge," a personal address to the ordinands, who stand to receive it. Some preachers omit the "charge" on the grounds that the homily should be addressed to all the people.

Following the sermon and Nicene Creed, the bishop delivers "The Examination," addressed to the ordinands. The address consists of two parts. The first part develops the theology of the diaconate in three sentences, on the Trinity, *diakonia*, and *agape*.

**1. My brothers and sisters,[4] every Christian is called to follow Jesus Christ, serving God the Father, through the power of the Holy Spirit.**

Source and model of all ministry, the Trinity sets the theological tone for what is to follow. In the famous icon by Andrei Rublev, "The Holy Trinity" (c. 1410), three angels, guests of Abraham and

103

✳

Sarah at the oaks of Mamre, sit around a meal in perfect love and harmony, clearly differentiated in body yet one in mind and heart and spirit. Their being is defined both by their personal attributes and by their relationships with each other. So it is, or should be, with the community of all Christians and their bishops, presbyters, and deacons. For all the baptized, the central commands are "follow" and "serve." Our baptismal calling is to follow Jesus and serve God the Father, and therein, with the help of the Spirit, we have our being.

Words about "service" appear three times in the opening sentences of the examination, and they have several meanings. To serve God—any or all three persons of the Trinity—has elements of both *agape* and *diakonia*; we love God, and we act for God. Thus the opening of the examination introduces a linguistic issue, the translation of ancient *diakon-* words, which has occupied several scholars during the past generation. How can one be precise in meaning and yet embrace a multitude of nuances? The issue may have been partly resolved, at least for the time being, by a lexicon of Greek in the New Testament and other early Christian writings. The 1979 edition of this standard work translated the verb *diakoneo* as: wait on someone at table; serve generally, of services of any kind; care for, take care of; help, support someone. The 2000 edition replaces these definitions with: function as an intermediary, act as go-between/agent; perform obligations; meet an immediate need, help; carry out official duties. The entries for *diakonia* and *diakonos* reveal similar changes.[5]

## 2. God now calls you to a special ministry of servanthood directly under your bishop.

The ancient and primary bond of deacons is with the bishop of the diocese—first the bishop who ordained the deacon, then that bishop's successors. If a deacon moves to another diocese, and the move is canonically approved through "letters dimissory" (a certificate from the bishop sending the deacon to another diocese), the bond transfers to the bishop of the new diocese.

The bond of deacons differs from the bond of priests. Priests work together with the bishop in a college of presbyters and hence take a "share in the councils of the Church." Other Christians gather around and work with the bishop, but they are free to come

104

✳

and go and function in all sorts of ways. They are accountable not directly to the bishop (with the exception of a few licensed ministries) but to the entire community of the baptized, and they also take part in the governance of the church. No statement in the Catechism or in the ordination liturgy gives deacons a formal conciliar role or grants them a vote in church governmental bodies. Absence of explicit permission, however, should not deny active deacons a vote in the democratic forums of the church, either by order or by election.

Because deacons are ordained to "a special ministry of servanthood," *diakonia* in which deacons act for the bishop, their role involves obedience to the bishop. It does not involve servility, passive acquiescence, or silence in the face of wrong. Deacons are subject, as persons in *diakonia*, to the bishop because the bishop oversees *agape* in the church. The ancient bond between deacons and bishop—by which the deacon acted as the eyes and ears of the bishop—does not translate easily into the twenty-first century. Today presbyters function much as bishops did in the third century, and much of the actual bonding is between deacons and presbyters. Deacons and bishops, however, seek new expressions of the ancient bonding that combine collegiality with discipline. Deacons thus help bishops to carry out their own ordination vow to "be merciful to all, show compassion to the poor and strangers, and defend those who have no helper."

**3. In the name of Jesus Christ, you are to serve all people, particularly the poor, the weak, the sick, and the lonely.**

As agents of the bishop, and hence of the church, deacons are responsible for a great variety of ministries in the church and the world. Deacons share these ministries with all the baptized, who aid the needy in many different ways; the difference is one of focus. Deacons are to be lights of ministry at the center of the church. One distinctive role of deacons is to hold up mercy and justice, just as they hold up the paschal candle in the midst of all the smaller, hand-held candles of the Easter Vigil, so that the people, led and encouraged by an example of radiance, will go into a world of darkness with candles of Christ.

Half a century ago deacons aided the needy mainly within the church: the poor, old, sick, and shut-in whom deacons visited and

to whom they brought the sacrament. There is precedent for this
form of ministry—the deacon of the early church who took the
sacrament directly from the Eucharist to Christians who could not
be present, especially those in prison. But early deacons such as
Laurence also found the poor in the world outside. In our age we
regard ministry to those within the church as primarily pastoral,
the work of the parish priest and certain other baptized persons; by
contrast, deacons now find the *anawim* in the world at large.
Poverty, weakness, sickness, and loneliness are global conditions,
too broad to be limited to the membership of the church. The
experience of Israel teaches us that recognition of poverty within
leads to recognition of poverty without. The bishop's instruction
"to serve all people" points through the church door to vast numbers outside.

In the second part of "The Examination" the bishop issues six
commands, each with "are to" verbs, on the life and work of deacons, and then asks seven questions requiring assent to aspects of
that life and work. Having told the ordinands they will act under
orders, the bishop gives the marching orders.

**1. As a deacon in the Church, you are to study the Holy
Scriptures, to seek nourishment from them, and to model
your life upon them.**

All ordained persons, and indeed all the baptized, are called to
holiness of life. The place to start is the Bible. Study, nourishment,
and modeling of Scripture are implied in the baptismal covenant
question about proclaiming the gospel "by word and example." Two
questions following the bishop's address to the ordinand indicate
the special importance of Scripture in the study and life of a deacon: "Will you be faithful in prayer, and in the reading and study of
the Holy Scriptures?" and "Will you do your best to pattern your
life [and that of your family, or household, or community] in accor-
dance with the teachings of Christ, so that you may be a whole-
some example to all people?" The bishop's address requires deacons
to study the scriptures but also to live as imitators of Christ.

The personal life of deacons should include the spiritual disci-
plines common to all Christians: daily prayer (especially the daily
office), family prayer (which includes all small groups), confession

of sin, and the Eucharist. The bishop's address also suggests that deacons adopt a program of regular, even daily, reading and study of Scripture and commentaries. Deacons may expand on this requirement by forming and leading groups to study the Bible.

The reason for this emphasis on the scriptures lies in the special role of the deacon as chief evangelist, the reader whose formal proclamation of the gospel encourages others to bear the Word into the world. The essence of Scripture is the *logos* or Word who is Christ. To study the Word is to feed on Christ. To model oneself on Christ is to adopt a life that is modest, simple, and humble. This is probably what the writer of 1 Timothy meant by saying that deacons "must hold fast to the mystery of the faith with a clear conscience" (1 Tim. 3:9). The mystery of the faith is the paschal mystery of Christ crucified and risen.

**2. You are to make Christ and his redemptive love known, by your word and example, to those among whom you live, and work, and worship.**

This statement bears on the symbolic nature of the diaconate. All Christians must relieve distress and seek out the causes of injustice; deacons are also symbols of Christ and his church. As we have seen, diaconal function gives life and structure to diaconal symbol. As agents of the church, deacons hold before it the whole ministry of the church as *diakonia* steeped in *agape*. As symbols of Christ, deacons reveal to the people of God that they all have been baptized as love-filled servants of the Lord.

As symbols of Christ, deacons occupy a special place in the *laos* as a living challenge to symbols of status and hierarchy. Although members of the clergy in canon law, they are also, in the ancient tradition of the church, members of the laity. In the account in *Apostolic Tradition*, the deacon "does not take part in the council of the clergy." The existence of deacons in the church raises profound questions about the historical development of the clergy (bishops and presbyters) into a professional estate above and separate from the vast majority of Christians. Deacons demonstrate that hierarchy or "sacred rule" does not have to be autocratic and superior; it can instead be participatory, embracing all as members of the councils of the church.

**3. You are to interpret to the Church the needs, hopes, and concerns of the world.**

Having walked in the world, deacons return to the church in the role of interpreter. This role has great value for the church, but first some qualification is necessary. By itself the bishop's direction to interpret the world to the church is not a license to preach. Preaching, whether by deacons or anyone else, is interpretation of the good news as it should be lived out in the world. It is a prescription for health. Deacons interpret the world in all its messiness to the church, because as workers among the needy, they have continual access to needs, concerns, and hopes. Other workers among the needy also have access, but only deacons are directed to *interpret*.

This means that deacons must be able to see and hear and speak. Part of the training of deacons should be to teach them languages and dialects in the broadest sense, what people mean when they speak in various ways. This talent involves skills in observation, listening, diagnosis, and speaking (including musical and artistic expression). It involves knowledge about how social and political systems, institutions, and organizations work. In a speech to a deacons' conference in 1989, Maylanne Maybee told of a social worker, preoccupied with Jungian psychology, who began her first interview with a client with "How do you feel?" The street person answered, "I feel *hungry*."

Maybee suggests three guidelines for listening and diagnosis: First, we must listen where others don't—"to children, to old people, to women, to street people, to natives, to people of color, to the voice of emerging nations." Second, we must voluntarily displace ourselves into situations not normal for us. Third, we must develop "the ability, the strength, and the willingness to make ourselves inconspicuous." These guidelines help us to be attentive to the needs, concerns, and hopes of the world in which we live and work.

Deacons interpret the world to the church in several settings. They interpret when they "make known to the bishop what is necessary," as *Apostolic Tradition* puts it. They interpret the world when they speak out in the forums of the church, and when they vote. They are expected to use their voice in conventions and on church bodies such as commissions and committees and vestries. In many parishes, deacons lead or work with outreach committees.

They interpret the world when they tell the stories and sing the songs and draw the pictures of the poor. In the liturgy, to "interpret" means to put the language of needs, concerns, and hopes into the language of bidding to prayer, as in the "prayers of the people." In the ancient language of the church at prayer, deacons are to list names and concerns of great need, so that the people can intercede through Christ to our Father in heaven.

**4. You are to assist the bishop and priests in public worship and in the ministration of God's Word and Sacraments.**

In the liturgy deacons act for the assembly in the role of deacon—as proclaimer of the gospel, interpreter of the world, and headwaiter at the table. The point of the diaconal role in liturgy is not that a subordinate assists the presider. The point is that a deacon, as a major performer in the assembly, plays a vital role in the complete action of the assembly. This performance does not take place in isolation, for the deacon works as part of a team of actors.

In the Christian liturgy, the people of God put on the masks of ancient Greek drama and bring about catharsis, sing the arias and duets and choruses of grand opera, kick up heels in a country dance, set fire and drown in water and rub oil and feed the hungry, perform for their own enjoyment and the pleasure of God. Liturgy is the closest experience of human beings to heaven on earth, and some say it is heaven. But I speak idealistically, with a sigh for the often grim reality.

Aidan Kavanagh, in a witty little book about liturgical style, says that the deacon is "the assembly's prime minister" who must be able to perform the other ministries as well as anyone else: "singer of singers, cantor of cantors, reader of readers . . . butler in God's house, *major domo* of its banquet, master of its ceremonies."[6] There are three activities in the liturgy in which the deacon performs as angel or table waiter: proclaimer of the gospel (angel), bidder of intercessions (both angel and table waiter, delivering messages and reading lists), and table waiter at the messianic banquet (setting the table, preparing the dishes, serving the food, making sure the banqueters don't make a mess, cleaning up, telling everyone to go home). Like every other action in liturgy, this is a matter of combining ancient tradition with local custom.

One complaint about deacons, especially from bishops and presbyters, concerns their bumbling and bungling in the liturgy. Cooking a pot of beans for a food program does not always translate into setting bread and wine on the eucharistic altar. Deacons need more help in liturgy than we have been giving them. Training should cover two areas: reading (including singing, a form of discourse that pleases God) and waiting on tables. Deacons need to learn to function in the choreographed, stylized liturgy of a cathedral as well as in an informal small setting. They need to learn to observe when help is needed—the bishop has lost his glasses!—and to spring to action at a crisis. Polite manners are equally proper in a hospital ward and a soup kitchen and a prison dining hall and the Christian liturgy. Learn to sing the Exsultet, gospel, prayers of the people, and dismissal (especially the Easter dismissal with alleluias). Even the tone deaf and others disabled in speech or hearing can be taught to make a joyful noise. Aidan Kavanagh writes: "A deacon who cannot sing is like a reader who cannot read, a presbyter (which means elder) without age or wisdom, a bishop (which means overseer) who cannot see, a presider who cannot preside."[7] It's a harsh judgment but all too often a true picture of what goes on.

110

If we train deacons to act in liturgy, we must also train bishops and presbyters to live and work with deacons, respecting their role and not stepping on their lines. We must remind the presider: stay away from the altar until your time arrives, and be a model of quiet prayer.

**5. And you are to carry out other duties assigned to you from time to time.**

Those who assign the unspecified other duties are mainly "the bishop and priests," a collective term for the collegial priesthood of the diocese, and perhaps also those presbyters who have legitimate but limited authority over the deacon, and the deacon must carry them out. Ordinands who take the bishop's address literally may be tempted to turn around and run out of church. The bishop may tell you to quit your job and get another, move to another town, move to another congregation, leave the hospital and enter prison, stop preparing babies for baptism and start collecting the dead for burial, leave the old folks' home and open a shelter for street addicts. Does this sound unreasonable? Most bishops will exercise common sense and pastoral good judgment. But if the instruction has any meaning, any force, it constitutes a binding agreement that the deacon is now at the service of the church to use for *diakonia*, wherever the bishop sees the need.

The instruction has another meaning. An order exists for the good of the community, not the good of the ordained minister. Here the bishop is warning ordinands against using the order for self. Deacons are ordained for others.

This statement is a variation of the vow of obedience, which the ordinand makes during the presentation. It is given its theological content by the last question following the bishop's address: "Will you in all things seek not your glory but the glory of the Lord Christ?" The deacon seeks God's glory by carrying out other duties assigned from time to time.

**6. At all times, your life and teaching are to show Christ's people that in serving the helpless they are serving Christ himself.**

The theological basis for this statement is Matthew 25:31–46. We are to feed the hungry, give something to drink to the thirsty, welcome the stranger, clothe the naked, care for the sick, and visit those who are in prison. Alongside the tabernacle in the sanctuary are temples of the Holy Spirit, the poor clamoring at the door for food, shelter, and a listening ear. Christ is present in all God's poor, and he can be found especially in those at the bottom of society. The distinct role of deacons in the church is to reveal the presence of Christ in the needy and helpless, and to carry this message to the people of God.

This is what the modern church means by deacons enabling, helping, and encouraging Christian people to serve. Deacons are to give Christian people the Christian reason to serve. Without the presence of Christ, ministry becomes institutional and impersonal, while the role of servant reverts to its secular meaning of low and mediocre status. In the liturgy the revelation of Christ in humanity occurs vividly when the deacon comes among the people and proclaims the good news of Christ to the poor in whom Christ dwells.

After the examination, with its concluding questions, the ordinands kneel facing the bishop, and all others stand while a hymn invoking the Holy Spirit is sung. This is almost always *Veni Creator Spiritus*. The Pentecost sequence *Veni Sancte Spiritus* is also permitted. Both hymns point to the invocation of the Spirit in the ordination prayer.[8]

After a period of silence, the bishop begins the prayer with an image of Christ drawn from the New Testament (my parentheses indicate sources):

> O God, most merciful Father,
> we praise you for sending your Son Jesus Christ,
> who took on himself the form of a servant, and
> humbled himself,
> becoming obedient even to death on the cross. (Phil. 2:7–8)
> We praise you that you have highly exalted him, and
> made him Lord of all;
> and that, through him, we know that whoever would be
> great must be servant of all. (Mark 10:44)
> We praise you for the many ministries in your Church,
> and for calling these your servants to the order of deacons.

Then the bishop lays hands on each ordinand in turn and prays over each:

> Therefore, Father, through Jesus Christ your Son, give
> your Holy Spirit to N;
> fill *him* with grace and power, and make *him* a deacon in
> your Church.

The bishop removes hands and concludes:

> Make them, O Lord, modest and humble, strong
> and constant,
> to observe the discipline of Christ.
> Let their life and teaching so reflect your commandments,
> that through them many may come to know you and
> love you. (Matt. 20:28)

> As your Son came not to be served but to serve, (Mark 10:45)
> may these deacons share in Christ's service,
> and come to the unending glory of him who, with you
> and the Holy Spirit,
> lives and reigns, one God, for ever and ever.

The prayer of the Canadian church uses similar scriptural and patristic sources but arranges them differently. I find the Canadian version more coherent and graceful in style, and there is one subtle but major theological difference. In the American version the bishop prays that the Father "make" the ordinand "a deacon in your Church." *God* consecrates. But in the Canadian version the bishop prays: "Send down your Holy Spirit upon your servant N, whom we now consecrate in your name to the office and work of a deacon in the Church." The Canadian prayer expresses the reality of the Spirit acting in and through the body of Christ. Empowered by God, *we* consecrate. In both the American and the Canadian prayers, only the Father is asked to give the fruits of consecration. A recent ordination prayer for deacons in the Church of England, apparently in response to the studies of Collins and others, correctly translates *doulos* in the passage from Philippians as "slave" and omits the inappropriate allusions to Mark.

Completing both prayer and ordination, the people shout "Amen" (the rubric says "in a loud voice"), and the deacon is vested with a stole worn over the left shoulder, and perhaps a dalmatic, as the distinctive vestments of the deacon. These may be worn in several ways, according to various ancient and medieval traditions. Vestments have nothing to do with personal adornment or status; they are the formal dress of the assembly, and the assembly should have a say in their design. They are beautiful costumes that attract the eye and capture the imagination, and emblems of dramatic parts conveying action. In "solemn" celebrations one sometimes still sees dress that suggests a performance of *The Mikado*. Contemporary vestments convey beauty through simplicity and honesty in fabric and shape. Does your dalmatic suggest and permit the active yet graceful movement of one who delivers messages and oversees meals? Is your stole visible? What should the messengers and angels wear at *this* wedding?

✳

The bishop then gives each new deacon a Bible—a remnant of the medieval *porrectio instrumentorum*, or "delivery of the instruments"—and says: "Receive this Bible as the sign of your authority to proclaim God's Word and to assist in the ministration of his holy Sacraments." In some dioceses the bishop also presents each new deacon with the book of gospels, equivalent to the giving of chalice and paten to a new priest. The sentence in the Roman Rite may be used: "Receive the Gospel of Christ, whose herald you now are. Believe what you read, teach what you believe, and practice what you teach." The giving of the Bible (and book of gospels) conveys the meaning of proclamation—deacon as angel and herald.

For the rest of the liturgy, the deacons perform their proper role at the table; if several have been ordained, they share the role. The bishop stays away from the altar until a new deacon finishes setting the table and preparing the food. Then the bishop comes to the table and censes the altar, if that is the custom, whereupon a deacon takes the censer and swings it toward and among the people—an angelic task—and the bishop begins the eucharistic prayer.

During the prayer one or two new deacons stand nearby, help the bishop follow the text, and protect the wine from spillage and insects. During the doxology, as the bishop lifts the bread, the deacon at the right side steps forward and raises the cup of wine in a gesture of offering. The new deacons then receive communion and afterward administer the sacrament in one or both kinds. Usually the bishop takes the bread and deacons the wine, but if there are several new deacons they may take both. After communion the bishop leaves the remaining sacrament on the altar and the deacons perform the ablutions. The rubrics suggest that the deacons remove the vessels, consume the remaining bread and wine, and clean the vessels "in some convenient place" (credence table or sacristy). A new deacon gives the dismissal, sending people out of the church, although normally they stick around for a reception.

After the liturgy, an ancient addition to the liturgy may take place. The deacons may carry the sacrament, both bread and wine, "to those communicants who, because of sickness or other grave cause, could not be present at the ordination." This obviously refers not to *nominal* Christians but to *faithful* communicants who would have been there if they could. I suggest that the new deacons publicly enlist eucharistic ministers to help in this extension of the body of Christ.

✳

The ordination and Eucharist inaugurate the deacons' ministry and set forth its meaning. In every Sunday Eucharist, in baptisms, and in the great liturgies of Holy Week and the paschal feast, the people learn through the drama of the liturgy that to be a Christian means to love and serve the Lord and to love their neighbors, including the poor. Their vow to uphold deacons in ministry includes upholding deacons in liturgical performance. The people are not passive listeners at a lecture on ethics, but part of the great drama of Christ on the cross. What they enact, they are. The old axiom *lex orandi, lex credendi* means: the law of prayer [is] the law of belief. Worship constitutes and forms belief. Liturgy forms the people of God in the life of Father, Son, and Holy Spirit.

Here is another axiom. Those who act in liturgy (especially those whom the church officially appoints) must also act in the work of *agape* and *diakonia* in the world. As Gail Ramshaw writes, "Simply said, here is the liturgical logic: that the weekly ritual of assembling around Christ in prayer for the world will form in Christian people the mind of praise and the habit of service."9 When one who works with the poor also proclaims the good news, calls on the people for prayers of compassion, and oversees table and meal, and the people recognize the connection between deacon's ministry without and deacon's ministry within, liturgy forms the people of God in Christian life.

✳

## CHAPTER EIGHT

# DEACONS AND THEIR STORIES

Rich as it is with symbol, ordination is only the beginning. In their life and work, in their congregations and in the world, in their collegiality and in their sharing of stories, deacons shape the meaning of their order. In this chapter, by telling their stories, twenty-five deacons contribute to an ongoing theological dialogue. These stories hold up a mirror image of what deacons are and what they do and what they expect to become. They reveal how deacons reflect on the nature of their calling, show how deacons model and encourage diaconal ministries for others, and provide a guide for those who call persons for ordination to the diaconate, as well as for those who are called. In these stories deacons speak for themselves.[1]

## KENNETH ARNOLD, DIOCESE OF MASSACHUSETTS (LIVING IN NEW YORK)

When I was discerning my vocation a dozen or so years ago, a good friend of mine who is a Roman Franciscan questioned my sense of diaconal calling. Knowing that I am a person in motion, he said, "You know, Ken, deacons are ordained to sit by the hearth. They stay home and tend the kitchen fires. You can't sit still." At first I thought he was right, and I spent a fair amount of time on the question of whether my naturally kinetic self might feel stifled in diaconal ministry. The more I thought about it, however, the more I came to believe that he was mistaken. Priests sit by the fire and take care of the homestead. Deacons are supposed to be in motion.

As my ministry has evolved, I have come to appreciate just how true that insight is. I spent two two-year periods in parish ministry, with different parishes, and then moved to Massachusetts to become director of communications. I assumed that the move to Massachusetts would be it for me. After this, retirement! But, to my considerable surprise, in October 2003 I became the publisher for Church Publishing, Inc., in New York City, departing Massachusetts almost exactly two years after I got there. The move is a good one for the church, and I feel that I have been called to it by the Holy Spirit. There was no real way to say no when I was invited to apply for the position.

When I began writing this article, one of the reasons to do it was to talk about what it means to be a deacon who actually works for a bishop. Although my boss at Church Pension Group, which owns Church Publishing, is not a bishop (in fact he is a West Point graduate), the new chair of the publishing board is retired Bishop Hays Rockwell. And so I continue to work closely with a bishop, although in a way that opens up perhaps richer possibilities for understanding the collaborative nature of deacon-bishop relationships. Bishop Rockwell is the chair of the publishing board but not my bishop. We are colleagues, each with authority in our own arenas, but we each have authority. That is, of course, what relationships between deacons and bishops should be like; our working relationship is close enough to be *experienced* as collegial. It is not abstract.

It is usually assumed that deacons will be assigned to a parish and that their ministry will be parish-based. There are good reasons for thinking that way. After all, the parish is the presumed base of Christian life. But if we think about diaconal ministry in light of the question raised by my Franciscan friend, it might be worth asking whether deacons should not be assigned to parishes (as a general rule) but should be working more broadly in the diocese or the church according to their particular skills and charisms. By placing deacons in parishes, we have restricted their movement, tying them more closely to parish life and to priestly visions of ministry than is natural for a healthy diaconal life. Deacons should not be tending the home fires. They should be on the road.

My friend is a Franciscan, part of that early movement that took monastics out of the cloister and put them on the road. Today, there are few in the church who see their ministries as being of the road. We speak of parish homes as places we never want to leave. Even the Franciscans are less mobile than they used to be. As I packed my bags to leave the Diocese of Massachusetts, I realized that movement is exactly what I need in order to live more fully into my vocation. I need to pack up and go, not out of some sense of personal need (or career development) but because that is the nature of my work. I go where the spirit sends me. (A life characterized by stability, so important to spiritual health, is still possible when motion is ordered by the spirit not by a restless flight from reality: what I am talking about is movement into not away from reality.)

When I was in New York previously, before moving to Massachusetts, one of the priests there often referred to me as Kenosis Ken. It was partly an acknowledgment of my practice of Zen meditation—and also I think she just liked the sound of it. Kenosis means emptying. I think it is a word that is particularly suited to the diaconal life, and closely related to a sense of diaconal ministry as ministry in motion. In opening ourselves to the call of the spirit to go and do the work we are given, we empty ourselves—that is, we give up our own assumptions about who and what we are. We allow ourselves to be empty to the moment. We also give up the assumptions that others have of us, even those bishops, priests, and laypeople we serve.

In Zen, there is an image of the self that is like a leaf (or, as some ancients say, duckweed) floating on a stream, going where it is taken—free and yet at the same time inextricably part of the flow of things. I cannot get out of the stream; and I don't try to remain stationary in the flow by clinging to a rock or the shore either. It is a good way to live, letting go, if it is done with awareness. For most of the deacons I know, it is also a hard way to live. We generally want to control our environment and everything in it. (At least, most of the deacons I know are like that. I know I'm that way.) And yet our vocation is to give up the illusion of control, to empty ourselves of what we think we are, to go where the spirit wills. That's who we are. And it isn't always comfortable for us or for the church.

## GARY BAIRD, DIOCESE OF ARKANSAS

I am a servant. It is not something that I set out to be but it is who I am. Let's call it God's gift to me. The environment that God set me in gave me experiences that led to this gift as well as my parents who taught me that people are important. So I can claim no honor in a disciplined life of effort to gain this gift. I am a servant by nature. My road to becoming a servant of servants is even less honorable, and I confess seems to be more because God was determined than I. So, here I am, waiting for my next blunder to become exactly what God wants me to do. Being a servant makes me happy. Being a servant of servants is challenging. But being the servant of the Servant gives me life.

A day in the life of this servant can be hectic. The way I feed myself and pay my bills is by being a gardener. I own my business and have a number of contracts. My wife is a teacher and between the two of us we manage. My contracts allow me flexibility in my hours so that I can intertwine ministry and work during the day. Stress is normally measured by how many showers I must take in a day as I move from gardens to meetings and occasionally in an emergency the shower is skipped and I do noonday prayers in my overalls. But that is so telling of a servant who is also a deacon in the church. The church and the world become so intertwined that the question of dress becomes unimportant. I surprise those who see me in a collar who knew me only in overalls, and in overalls who knew me only in a collar. Many a holy conversation has come from such meetings.

People ask me how being a deacon has changed my ministry. I reply, "It hasn't." Remember I am a servant by nature. I would still see people as the reason for the gospel message. I would still reach out to those who are kept from hearing it. I would still annoy the church with reminders of who they are missing. My retort would be, "I think the real question is: How is the ministry of the church different because this servant is a deacon? And what changes in the world because of that?" The answer has something to do with overalls and collars and doors that allow both to pass through. A member of my congregation who worked at an institute for the deaf brought to church youth from the institute, and signed the liturgy for them. After one service I went up to thank her for her wonderful ministry, and she dismissed the thank-you by saying it was not really ministry, only her job. She was teaching them how to sign "church words." I told her to feel free to bring her work to church and the church to her work anytime she wanted. She looked surprised but smiled. I think she was one step closer to understanding that she was a servant too.

## BETTY BELASCO, DIOCESE OF LONG ISLAND

My work as a chaplain at Ground Zero was the hardest task I have ever experienced, but also the most rewarding. Housed in the temporary morgue, I was notified as remains were found. Along with one or more emergency medical technicians, I went to the Pile (later to become the Pit) to pray over the remains. Then I returned to the temporary morgue where careful records were prepared in the presence of an assistant medical examiner, a police photographer, and often members of the various services (NYPD, FDNY, PAPD). During this time I offered additional prayers such as the commendation. If the remains were identified as of a member of service, I said the commendation at the foot of the ramp as members of all services at Ground Zero stood at attention on the ramp. This service was broadcast throughout Ground Zero, and all present stood in silence during that time. At all times, all workers were outfitted with respirators, goggles, hard hats, etc., and were cautioned to be alert to ground debris and large machinery whose operators could not always see the individuals—and this was often while slogging through the muck. Whenever it was a particularly bad day, God sent some humor down to me—such as the time the EMTs in the morgue discovered how old I was (71 at the time), and suddenly the "every man for himself" rule was out, and they treated me like a fragile old lady. That lasted for one day!

Currently, I am serving as chaplain (non-denominational or anything else) at Memorial Park, where the unidentified remains from people reported as missing from 9/11 and not yet identified are held, pending DNA. Memorial Park is located at the Chief Medical Examiner's Office, and families and friends come to visit, pray, leave flowers, stuffed toys, letters, and other memorabilia. I am there to support visitors and staff. Each time I go (once a week), I pray over each person by name. And I pray for each of their families and friends that they may receive comfort from the Holy Spirit. Dr. Hirsch, who is Chief Medical Examiner, is very emphatic that each of those lost ones be supported by us in prayer. That, in itself, gives me heart to continue in this ministry.

## BARB BISHOP, DIOCESE OF CHICAGO

When I was ordained on the Feast of St. Ambrose 1991, the preacher, Faith Perrizo, described the ways in which deacons, by use of their talents, can be icons of God. She had a particular icon in mind for each of the eight ordinands. Mine was: "Deacons offer an icon of God as one who brings order out of chaos. Deacons willingly step into chaotic situations and quietly bring sense and order that we may better enjoy God." Faith's characterization of me was right on target. I am always the one who asks who, what, where, when, how, and how much.

In 1989 I started a nursing home ministry on behalf of our church. One situation of chaos, but one of my great joys, was ministering to an Episcopal priest and his mother. She was in her 80s, and he was in his mid-50s, stricken with multiple sclerosis and wheelchair bound. After a time of building up rapport with him, I was able to have him help out (with much assistance) at special liturgies. What a delight to see the look on his mother's face as he placed the Ash Wednesday ashes on her forehead! Another time, I arranged for him to celebrate the Eucharist for a small group. A eucharistic minister from St. Mary's assisted, and we managed to get him vested and led him through the celebration. I felt honored that we could do this so he could validate his ministry as a priest.

As he lay near death a few years later, I was called to the hospital. Our rector was on vacation, and so I gave his sister the option of calling in another priest. But she wanted me to anoint him. It turned out that I was the last one to anoint him, and he was the first person that I ever anointed. It was an amazing time of grace!

A good portion of my time and ministry the last three years has been to my parents. Both of them are in a nursing home. My brother and I have tried to honor their wishes for independence while still getting the best medical care for them. We have also been maintaining their house. But it is clear that their days of independence are over and we are now in the process of selling it. This has been a stressful time for all of us, but also a time of much grace. I have discovered that as we have been ministering to our parents, they have been ministering to us as well. This experience has enabled me to be a diaconal icon to others dealing with aging parents.

## JACQUIE BOUTHÉON, DIOCESE OF TORONTO

"You have to move in six months. This home is closing." Terrifying words to forty-three seniors aged 80 to 103 years old, some of whom moved in recently, some of whom "came with the furniture" over twenty years ago. Once again, economic reasons and business issues have won out over the welfare of our most vulnerable citizens: the frail elderly.

As coordinating chaplain to the long-term care facility, and as a volunteer worker for over eleven years, I had come to know all the residents well and was personally shocked to receive the news in a voicemail message. In one sense I dreaded going there that Saturday evening to officiate at the Service of Light and prepare the chapel for the next morning's Eucharist. In another sense I felt that was exactly where I was needed—and where I needed to be. The management had not taken the trouble to call either the senior chaplain or the priest of the parish church across the courtyard to be present when they announced the news to the residents. Fearful of leaks, they had also decided to inform family members at the same time the residents were being told, instead of in advance so they could be present.

So began the process of helping these seniors to work through their feelings and to start the administrative hurdles to be crossed in an attempt to find facilities. Some wanted to stay in the area because of families and friends, some had to face the decision to move further away to be closer to those families and friends.

In this time of upheaval and distress, it became essential to ensure that spiritual supports were there for the residents. We organized some of the clergy who had taken services in the past, or who still took them, to form a team whose members would be available to residents and their families.

There was also advocacy work to do, talking to residents and families about the places they were considering, reassuring them about the availability of worship services and spiritual care. As the residents found places in other long-term care facilities, I was able with the assistance of our diocese and the national church to discover the closest Anglican parish and notify the clergy that one of our residents was moving into that parish. By doing this in person by telephone, I was able to explain the background, so that the clergy would understand any feelings of anger or frustration expressed to them. In every case I was assured that the new residents would be visited shortly and that their spiritual needs would be taken care of.

The closing was announced at the end of September, effective at the end of the following March. In January I arranged for the area bishop to come and celebrate our Sunday Eucharist. One of the

123

✳

gospel choices for that Sunday was the wedding feast at Cana. The bishop reassured them that "even if the wine appears to have run out, the best wine is being kept for last." The presence of the bishop did much to encourage the residents who were left.

Still, a sense of disbelief continued to be present, until the first resident moved away. Then the realization set in that this was for real, and that this separation was only the first of many. As the residents scattered to new homes, it was difficult for those left behind to realize that the home was indeed to be closed and that in many cases they would not see their friends again.

Through what I learned in helping one of my close friends who lived there to find a new home, I was able to help other families to avoid some of the pitfalls inherent in the choice of a new institution. Thirteen residents chose the same new home, which was to open in early March. They, together with the budgie,[2] were the first residents to move in. Although strictly speaking some of them should have been placed on the medical floor, the staff decided to keep them all together in the same unit. After learning that the parish priest could only commit to one Eucharist a month (a sorry replacement for twice a week!), the senior chaplain undertook to celebrate the Eucharist the other weeks. I also became involved, especially in helping those I knew so well to get over the strangeness of a new facility.

Coming to the new facility with my friends has opened up a whole larger ministry, as I have become known to the staff and residents. Even though most of what I do is not in a liturgical role, I am known as a deacon and have been called to more than one deathbed to administer communion and help the family. I have also assisted some residents with articulating and writing down their own wishes for their funerals, so that "the kids will do it right." To these frail seniors who for the most part can no longer go outside the facility, particularly to church, I am able to bring the presence of the church.

## PHINA BORGESON, DIOCESE OF NORTHERN CALIFORNIA

Early this year I had an illuminating few moments sorting out how I was relating to a number of folks in ministry. I was frustrated with the seminary, but realized I needed to be there when I could to encourage the students who were looking toward work in ministry development. I was happy with my travels to the Shared

Ministry congregations here in Northern California, and with my interactions with those working on the Shared Ministry program. I was frustrated in my parish, where I seemed to spend a lot of energy tending to inertia. So there I was, at the Sunday Eucharist, thinking about how my relationship with Alan Scarfe was going to change now that he was becoming Bishop of Iowa. How would I support him in his ministry in this changed relationship? I was also thinking about Bill Pease, one of the members of my congregation, with whom I had gone to the peace march in San Francisco the day before. I don't like crowds, but it seemed important to support this Vietnam veteran, to join him in his stand against war. And then it dawned on me: supporting others in their ministries is an incredible privilege. It is the greatest gift I have been given, the opportunity to be with others, to encourage and challenge as they serve in the name of Christ. I realized, too, that my discomfort at some of the ministry support I am called to offer is because in supporting a person I also sometimes fall into the trap of supporting structures that confine, constrain, and limit the ministry of all believers.

The other side, then, of the tremendous joy and privilege of supporting others in ministry—something I believe all church leaders are called to do—is removing barriers and working for structural change. Clearing away the barriers strikes me as intensely diaconal.

Once at a staff retreat when I was working for the Diocese of Los Angeles as education missioner, the proper for the Eucharist was the feast of William Augustus Muhlenberg. The gospel is Matthew's account of the cleansing of the temple. I saw vividly Jesus' action, but also all the things we in the church do to re-erect barriers and clutter people's pathways to the holy. Doing my best to keep access open and barrier free became a metaphor for my ministry. In my congregation, it meant challenging those who didn't mind that we ate dinner with the poor on Wednesday evenings, but who didn't want them in church on Sunday morning. At the office it meant improving communication with those responsible for Christian education in the parishes, opening up knowledge of the resources of the wider church for them; the mail that stops on the rector's desk is one of the biggest barriers to ministry we face. In my work with Hispanic and Asian ministries it meant training Bible study leaders in multilingual conferences, so that any small group could approach scripture confidently, without the mediation of a professional leader. In my work with the commission on lay min-

125
❋

istry it meant promoting programs that raised awareness of ministry in daily life and helped groups and congregations organize to support it, so they could do some of their own barrier clearing.

Having taken to heart the Robert Greenleaf axiom that servant leaders are those who enable others to become servant leaders, I realized that a large part of deacon dirty work is removing the barriers that prevent others from claiming Christ's empowerment. Thus, by calling, I am myself a ministry developer. But there is also the persistence of the interpretation clause in the ordinal, which triggered my inner response to the call to be a deacon.

A large chunk of my current ministry is working for the National Center for Science Education, a non-profit membership organization committed to "defending the teaching of evolution in the public schools." I am the Faith Network project coordinator, which means that I work with people of faith who support the teaching of evolution in our public schools. As a by-product of building the network, I have been privileged to participate in a number of programs and meetings engaged in the dialogue between science and theology. Involvement in those dialogues is, to me, a part of my diaconal ministry of interpretation.

One of my frustrations, though, is that so much of the dialogue is held captive in the academy, the province of men (mostly) with advanced degrees in science or theology or, often, both. Little is done to bring the dialogue into the church. For most folks in our congregations, even if they would deny being fundamentalists when it comes to the first few chapters of Genesis, the theology of creation they sing and preach and pray is thoroughly uninformed by contemporary science. Few church leaders have the background in science to facilitate ethical conversations about genetic engineering, the environment, or the impact of scientific progress on understanding the nature of humanity. Most don't even know how to begin asking questions of those in their congregations or communities who might have the necessary knowledge base.

I have begun to work on developing resources that might help this situation. But I also realize that the work of interpretation, particularly when one is interpreting to the church the concerns of a community with which it historically (at least in the last few centuries) has not had a close relationship, means first cultivating the audience that might want to hear. A church preoccupied with institutional maintenance and issues of personal morality is not poised

126
❋

to receive diaconal interpretations of broader societal, or even cosmic, concerns.

### TOM BRADSHAW, DIOCESE OF ARKANSAS

Prison ministry was never a personal objective. I could never have imagined working in that setting until after I had been there. After my Cursillo experience, I wanted to share the good news of God's love with others, and I searched without success for months for opportunities to share. In the meantime, a friend persisted in inviting me to serve with him in the Kairos Prison Ministry, but I declined each time. I thought, "There are bad people in there, and I certainly don't want to risk injury." As it turned out, I couldn't have been farther from the truth.

One day I listened closely to a song on my tape deck, a song titled "Kyrie." One of the verses caught my attention, and I played it over and over. The verse was, "Walk among them, I'll go with you—reach out to them with my hand. Suffer with me, and together we will serve them, help them stand." I realized then that this was my invitation to walk with Christ in prison. I called my friend and accepted the invitation to serve with him on Arkansas Kairos No. 2, Pine Bluff Unit.

The first time I walked into the prison, the gate at the sally port clanged shut behind me. I looked up at the razor wire coiled at the top of the chain-link fence, and I realized this was serious business. As I passed through the corridor into the chapel area, I looked at the bars surrounding me and, for a fleeting moment, felt trapped. I realized that I was locked in and that my freedom was at the mercy of the correctional officers at each barred gate. It was a new feeling, and I didn't like it.

Once inside the chapel, I forgot about the bars outside, and I met the chaplain and his assistants. The assistants were prisoners, all dressed in white uniforms with their names stenciled on their shirts. They were pleasant and friendly, and I soon forgot about being locked inside a prison. As the day progressed, I met other prisoners who had come to the chapel for the weekend Kairos retreat. They were standoffish at first, but they soon relaxed and we exchanged names and other personal information. As we introduced ourselves, they told us why they had come to Kairos, and we told them why we had come. Most of the prisoners said they had come for the food and "something different," and most of the volunteers said they had come to watch God work in this environment. I didn't know what to expect, because I had only experienced God in a friendly environment, and this definitely didn't seem to be friendly.

As the weekend progressed and we made new friendships, I forgot about the bars and confinement. It was a surprise on Sunday afternoon when, as I stood in the barred corridor outside the chapel, I suddenly realized again that I was trapped inside a prison, but this time I didn't worry. I simply smiled and reminded myself that God was with me and that I was surrounded by friends, both free world and inmates, and I wasn't concerned anymore. I had discovered a brand new world, and it was inhabited by people who understood love and forgiveness. I understood then what it means to be free even when locked up.

After ten years, I sometimes think it's odd that I feel so at home in prison. I started as a lay volunteer and served six years in that capacity, but it wasn't enough. I felt the tug of the Holy Spirit pulling me to participate to a greater extent. The bishop agreed that I could serve more fully as a deacon, so I pursued that goal. Once I was ordained, I returned to the familiar prison environment in a new role—as a spiritual director on a Kairos team. That opened new doors for me with the inmates, because they saw me in a different light, and they sought different responses. Sometimes I don't feel as though I'm prepared enough, but more likely than not, I feel grateful that I'm more prepared than I once was. There is so much need, and so few to respond.

In God's wisdom, he led me to a new opportunity this year. The prison in which I had been working with a small group to teach the Episcopal tradition lost its medical administrator, and the contractor was searching for an experienced medical administrator. As providence would have it, the search led them to me, and two days later I was hired. Even though the position has required some adjustments on my part to serve inside the prison in a different capacity, the Holy Spirit has not forsaken me—I now have the opportunity to love them both as their healthcare manager and as spiritual counselor. It is humbling and gratifying to have that opportunity.

## JOANNE DAUPHIN, CONVOCATION OF AMERICAN CHURCHES IN EUROPE

As the first deacon in our jurisdiction, I'm working only for the bishop (Pierre W. Whalon), not yet (if ever) assigned to a parish. My assignments are working with entirely French (officially designated) missions in Toulon and Bordeaux and with French-speaking African refugees, mostly Rwandan Anglicans, in Rennes (Brittany). Another mission is continued and enhanced ecumenical work.

In Paris we cannot separate the local (parish), citywide, national, European, and even worldwide aspects. For the last ten years or so, I've been cathedral delegate to our local ecumenical association, now twenty-one parishes around the Champs-Elysées. Four of these parishes are also cathedrals—ours, the Russians, the Greeks, and the Armenians. So we are also implicated in (expatriate) national-level figures, including, for one, the head of all the Orthodox in France. The new rector of one of the Roman Catholic local parishes is also city-wide ecumenical delegate for Cardinal Archbishop Lustiger. And one of the French Reformed Church pastors is also national chair of all Lutherans and Reformed Church people in France. Culturally, this seems very normal here, since so much is still centralized in Paris in the secular and political fields as well.

The president of our local ecumenical association is a Roman Catholic permanent deacon, an industrialist, married with teenaged children. My own ordination to the diaconate in 2003 was attended by national and local ecumenical figures, including Roman Catholic and Orthodox, and it has, if anything, enhanced my opportunities to be effective at the local level, and perhaps the diocesan as well. I am part of the Anglican delegation to the French ARC which is headed by a local English rector (also part of our local ecumenical association).

My impressions after ten years: in our particular setting (with many expatriate congregations of various denominations, as well as the French Roman Catholics and Protestants) ecumenism is alive and well at the personal and parish level. The further one goes "up" in the hierarchy, the more complicated it becomes. But in any event, the overwhelming majority of people who turn up at events (worship, lectures, etc.) are grey haired or the equivalent! Expats, especially short-term ones, have too much else on their plates, I surmise. For instance, in our cathedral parish, I imagine virtually all families

129

are "mixed" in terms of denomination and often also in terms of nationality. So one doesn't necessarily need to go to a meeting to "do" ecumenism. I have been in an ecumenical bicultural marriage for forty years.

Our convocation increasingly emphasizes, along with other missions, work with youth. I do not perceive any particular interest among youth in ecumenism, although they just naturally network with other, particularly English-speaking youth, "organized" or not. Taizé is a wonderful resource, but probably the ecumenical aspect is not the most important for most young pilgrims. Ecumenism is an imperative, not an option, so let's just try to carry on—with, we hope and pray, the help of the Spirit!

## Susanne Watson Epting, Diocese of Iowa (living in New York)

The late retired Bishop of Alaska, George Harris, was always quick to point out that the renewal of the diaconate occurred at the same time as the renewal of our understanding of the centrality of baptism. Indeed, that may be the single most important thing about the grounding of who I am as a deacon.

Some of my formation was rooted in my attendance at a meeting in 1981 at Notre Dame, where I had the privilege of meeting the late Bishop Wes Frensdorff and Deacon Phina Borgeson, among others. This meeting was sponsored by the Centre for the Diaconate (then in Boston) and others. It provided a foundation upon which my understanding of the diaconate, specifically, and ministry in general, has rested now for more than twenty years. While it would still be another eight years before I was ordained, a glimpse of a theology of ministry rooted in baptism would, along with the Holy Spirit, on some days keep my nose to the grindstone, and on others provide the excitement and vision of a church in which the diaconate was appreciated both for its prophetic and interpretive role, and as a way for us to be reminded of the servant nature of Christ's church and the *diakonia* of all believers.

I was privileged to encounter a commission on ministry who, rather than set the diaconate aside for lack of understanding, became willing partners in restoring it. And I was privileged to be ordained by a bishop whose legacy has been trust and mutuality.

The context here is important. It doesn't happen that way for everyone. Of course, there were obstacles. Of course, there were frustrations. Of course, there were setbacks. But I firmly believe that, in this day, part of my call to the diaconate is to help others understand it—from a position of strength. This context is important for me to describe because it has influenced everything about what it means to me to be a deacon.

My first "letter of agreement" with a congregation was really a covenant that reiterated the baptismal covenant. What the commission on ministry was looking for was more of a job description. My little congregation spoke about the meaning of the baptismal covenant in everyday life and the diaconate in relation to that. And while the work I've done and am doing is part of my story and a way to understand some of the roles that deacons play, it's important to articulate this grounding, this context, as strongly as space allows.

We're still asking, "What is your diaconal ministry?" And we'll still discover that the peculiarity of the diaconate allows for us all to live that in different ways. Many different ways, and yet we all promise the same things.

While I could say that I worked in an HIV clinic, that I advocated for a sane AIDS policy at the state legislature, that I served as resource person for the diocesan human needs commission, that I trained eucharistic visitors and those who prepared prayers of the people, the overarching themes and venues of ministry have been in ministry development and in asking the church to examine the obstacles to being a servant structure.

Those themes have been lived out as a canon to the ordinary, as a deployment officer, a spiritual director, a community developer; in teaching, preaching, and articulating, in the best way I know how, the intersection between spirituality and culture, the connection between being in love with God and kneeling to wash the feet of those unlike us; the ever-emerging realization of how glorious it is when we recognize the difference between identifying needy people and reaching down to them and identifying the gifts of all people and inviting them into friendship in Christ.

What I "do" now is humbling. A community of peers invited me to become executive director of the North American Association for the Diaconate—people I've looked up to over the years, who have given years and years of their lives to make the diaconate a reality, inviting the church to bring the edges to the center. So I am a deacon among deacons. I look for ways for deacons to be represented in the church, for programs to be made available that will strengthen diaconal ministry for deacons and others. I invite the church to dismantle things that get in the way of mutuality, servant leadership, and mission in the world. I write prayers and meditations as a way to remain connected with the diocese in which I am canonically resident. I am an itinerant of sorts, grounded by a community that extends around the nation, liturgically active as appropriate in the many places I travel, and supported by a covenant group and a clearness committee. And I pray for deacons everywhere and give thanks for the gift of Christ the Servant.

### ROBERT ANTON FRANKEN, DIOCESE OF MISSOURI

Coming up on twenty years of ordination to the diaconate hardly seems possible, but it's true. The stories of those years are many and varied, from lobbying to administration, from the corporate to the religious, from a wheelchair to walking, from Anchorage to Denver to Saint Louis—these are the many chapters of my life as a deacon. Most recently, in an attempt to blend the various pieces of my life and to utilize the eclectic mix of education, experiences, and talents that God has given me, I created Strataventure, LLC.

The story begins as my wife, Nancy Kinney, was finishing her doctoral dissertation in late 2000, and I was employed as the chief administrative officer for the Diocese of Colorado by Bishop William Jerry Winterrowd. Four years earlier, when she started back to school for her Ph.D., I promised that when she finished her degree we would move to wherever she found a job that she wanted, as long as it had a large body of water and a major airport. Well, Saint Louis has a large body of water, the Mississippi (I forgot to specify how wide it had to be), and at that time a major airport (with the recent American Airline cuts that is not nearly as certain). Nancy accepted a position as an assistant professor with the University of Missouri at St. Louis.

Six months later, in the middle of summer, we moved. I followed my wife as the trailing spouse into a diocese (Missouri) that had only two deacons, one of whom was retired, and a bishop who was unsure what to do with deacons. Bishop Hayes Rockwell, the ninth Bishop of Missouri, was intrigued by my talents and experience and, although unwilling to deploy me into a congregation, did afford me the opportunity to open my own consulting company.

Less than four weeks after we had arrived, in a lunch conversation we began talking about a non-profit conference center operated on land owned by the bishop in trust for the diocese. The conference center was losing money and needed some outside expertise to evaluate its viability. Would I be interested? This job became the first client of a rapidly formed company called Strataventure, LLC, which opened August 2001, three weeks before 9/11.

My goal in creating a for-profit management company was to provide organizational management, event management, consulting, and training to all kinds of organizations, but to use the profits of the corporate clients to subsidize the work we would do for faith-based clients. Unfortunately or fortunately, the corporate work we had hoped for was dramatically slowed down by the economy following 9/11, but we have maintained a steady stream of work from faith-based entities over the last three years. Slowly we are developing the corporate base we will need for long-term viability.

Each day that I work with faith-based clients, analyzing their systems to make them more efficient, accountable, and "nimble," or work to create an experiential event; or provide leadership training or coaching—I know that I am fulfilling my diaconal role by making the church more able to reach into and serve the world into which God has placed it.

In addition, with the consecration of the tenth Bishop of Missouri, George Wayne Smith, there has been a renewed commitment to the revitalization of the diaconate in Missouri. Under the new bishop and with the appointment of a new dean, Ronald C. Clingenpeel, I was assigned to Christ Church Cathedral in St. Louis to live out my liturgical role as non-stipendiary deacon. Life is good, and God is great here in St. Louis. I wonder what God has in store for me next?

## JOYCE HARDY, DIOCESE OF ARKANSAS

I had been to Cursillo and felt that God was calling me to . . . something. I wasn't sure what that something was, but when I told others about this stirring, they said that God must be calling me to the priesthood. After all, I was very active in the small church in my hometown, showing up whenever the doors were open. I was the senior warden and was very interested in everything about the

133

Episcopal Church. So I responded to that call, going to several committees to help me in the discernment process in Oklahoma. I began some studying, went for my psychological and physical exams, and started making plans to go to seminary. I was miserable. I stumbled when people asked me why I felt called to the priesthood. What else could God be calling me to do and be? Every meeting, every interview, every seminary brochure felt like I was running into a wall. I decided to put my process on hold. Surely God couldn't be calling me into such misery.

During this interim time, I talked with Bishop Cox, our assistant bishop who had recently come from the Diocese of Maryland. He asked me why I felt called to the priesthood. I was beginning to understand that I wasn't. Then he asked me to consider that the call may be to the diaconate. Since I didn't know what that was, he invited me to visit a group of people who were exploring the diaconate. As I listened to them, I got excited! They were talking about things that gave me energy: working with those who felt marginalized, getting others to help respond to the needs in the world. Then I went to a Province VII conference on the diaconate and met Ormonde, Phina, and other deacons. This must be what the call was all about.

I entered the deacon formation program in Oklahoma as a part of the first class. Through that process, my call and the diaconate became clearer. I was ordained deacon in 1985 and was moved from my home church to explore where I needed to be in the Tulsa area, as I had recently accepted a position at the Episcopal school in Tulsa.

When I moved to Arkansas four years later, I knew that there were no deacons and no deacon formation program, but I hoped that I might get something started. That didn't happen for several years. Although there were some deacons who had moved from other dioceses, I was assured that there would be no real acceptance of deacons in the near future. It was a very lonely time; two other deacons and I got together to talk "deaconese" on a fairly regular basis.

When we were interviewing for a new bishop, we made sure that questions about deacons were asked. We elected Larry Maze, a priest from Mississippi, who had had virtually no experience with deacons but had been on a committee to study the diaconate in that diocese. He asked for the commission on ministry to decide whether we would have a deacon formation program in the Diocese of Arkansas. After hearing a presentation by my friend and mentor from Oklahoma, Rick Brewer, the commission enthusiastically endorsed the diaconate. We carefully put together a competency-based program. I continue to direct the program, with the help of very supportive examining chaplains and a strong community of deacons.

I continue to form my theology of the diaconate. I have come to realize that most of what I do is baptismal ministry; when I serve others in any way, I am simply trying to keep my baptismal covenant. My diaconal ministry is involved when I'm out "looking for trouble" in my community, when I try to help others recognize the gifts they have to respond to that "trouble," and when I advocate for those who do not believe that their voice is heard.

I have worked with victims of violence, with at-risk youth, with people who are poor, hungry, and homeless, with persons with AIDS, with those who are illiterate or who need help with their English, with persons who have mental or physical disabilities, and with those who are imprisoned. It's when I'm connecting these people with people in the church that I'm really doing diaconal ministry.

There are two questions that I believe are very important in the discernment process if one feels called to ordained ministry. The first is "How will ordination enhance my ministry?" For the most part, those who are passionate about justice issues will continue to minister in those areas whether they are ordained or not. But the second question, "How will ordination enhance the ministry of the church?" must be examined and answered.

Although formation of skills, knowledge, and identity is necessary, one can't learn the passion required to be a deacon. One Sunday one of the members of the children's choir leaned over to one of the adult leaders and said, "When I grow up, I want to do what Joyce does."

"You mean," responded the adult, "that you want to read the gospel, set the table, and dismiss the congregation."

"No," the child responded, "I want to work with poor people."

She understood what it means to be a deacon.

135

## LYNNE HOUGH, DIOCESE OF MISSISSIPPI

I was ordained to the diaconate on February 18, 1996. Sometimes it seems like only yesterday, and sometimes it seems like I've been a deacon forever. That cold winter night when I received the laying on of hands by the bishop and invocation of the Holy Spirit with the words, "Make her a deacon in your church," my life was changed for ever.

This was the culmination of two years of formal classroom work with three classmates and myself. We would go our separate ways. One to work in a parish with inner-city ministry. One to work in a prison with death row inmates. One to work with unwed mothers. And me to the hospital chaplaincy. In addition to the time of discernment and formal school for deacons I had also done five units of Clinical Pastoral Education in preparation for the hospital chaplaincy. At the time of my ordination I had served two years as a lay chaplain. A hospital chaplain is privileged to have a more pastoral role than the average deacon ordinarily has.

My hospital is a large, full-service, not-for-profit hospital. Our patients range from the most affluent to the poverty-stricken, and we are the hospital who treats them all. At any given time I may be with the tiniest of the tiny in the neo-natal intensive care unit—offering comfort there to the little ones or their parents or especially the staff who care so much when little lives hang in the balance. Or I may be in more traditional intensive care units, such as cancer units for children and adults, trauma units, rehab units, or stroke and orthopedic units. We have 400 beds, and I don't even know how many square feet we're building all the time. I'm everywhere all the time, but I'm doing what God has called me to do, and it's the best feeling in the world, and I wouldn't do or be anywhere else.

Someone once asked me, "Is all you do just visit the sick?" I said, "Yes." But it's so much more. It's letting folks talk about fears and frustrations. It's letting them talk about their anxiety about having their chest cracked open and having a mere man holding their heart in his hand. It's about being afraid to die and saying it out loud and having someone to say it to. It's about saying, "Jesus loves you."

## THALIA JOHNSON, DIOCESE OF MICHIGAN

Raised an Episcopalian in a small town in Michigan, it wasn't until I moved to the Upper Peninsula in 1977 that I first began to comprehend the role of the church in social action. The first women had just been ordained as priests; the wife of our priest was the mayor of the city and had started the first women's center at the local university. Inclusive language and gay rights were other topics actively discussed there in the church. In 1982 with another job transfer I moved to Adrian, Michigan, near the Ohio border, and the first Sunday visited the local Episcopal church. That was the first time seeing a woman at the altar and the first time seeing a deacon. I don't remember even hearing of deacons in the Episcopal Church before that day. I later learned she was in the process toward priesthood.

As a teenager in the 1960s with parents who worked with people from around the world and discussed current issues at home, the civil rights movement was a strong influence. That eventually led to three years as a Peace Corps volunteer in Malaysia. Work back here as an Extension 4-H youth agent in rural counties helped reinforce the need for anti-racism education. The church in Adrian had an active ministry with the Hispanic population and with those in need. The local clergy involved me immediately in youth programs and six months later invited me to attend diocesan convention as a visitor. During a dinner there one of our lay delegates asked me out of the blue when I was going to start the process to become a deacon. It was a defining moment. As someone who never perceived herself either as very spiritual or as remotely gifted for ministry it was also a shock. At the same time, though, it felt like that was what all the previous experiences had been leading toward. I stayed up a good part of the night with the deacon asking questions. What did this mean? A strong part of the decision to enter discernment was the opportunity the church provided via the diaconate to be active in social justice issues while maintaining the neutral stance I perceived was required as a government employee. There was never any call to priesthood.

Studies began in January 1983 through the Whitaker School of Theology, and ordination took place in September 1987. During this time the description of a deacon as a channel through which the needs of the community and the resources of the church interacted became a strong focus. Clientele in the workplace became aware of the study program and were very supportive, even some who felt no need to be connected with a faith community. Quietly they brought word of families in need, and we found resources.

✳

That continued after ordination and the dual roles in the community intersected even more frequently.

While involved in specific programs with the Hispanic Community in 4-H, several people spoke over several years of the desire to do anti-racism work more intentionally, especially with youth. Upon retirement in 1996 nine of us created Cambios, Inc., a local non-profit organization dedicated to eliminating racism in Lenawee County by providing educational resources and programs. I served as the president and director for the first four years, having both the time and the financial freedom. It was the focus of my diaconal ministry, and all involved were aware of that commitment. To date Cambios (Spanish for "changes") has provided fifty different multicultural children's books to all twenty-six elementary schools and thirteen libraries in the county.

In one small community two years ago a high school senior who was in training to be a reader asked about his father's prejudice towards African Americans. Recently an eighth grader asked essentially the same question about the African American author of one of the Cambios books. The question is difficult and an indicator of the need for anti-racism programs, yet it is also incredibly hopeful to have a student that young asking it. The church has been supportive of Cambios. Both the parish and Diocese have given financial gifts and our diocesan newspaper has provided helpful coverage.

Community intersections continue to be a joy and tension for me as an older deacon. Diversity training and issues that bring the most challenge to the church currently keep me convinced that deacons are desperately needed. Members of target groups, those most marginalized, are raising voices in greater numbers and volume, calling for authentic relationships. Deacons are the icons of the most authentic relationship available to us all, God with people, through Jesus Christ.

## JOHN LeSUEUR, DIOCESE OF NEW HAMPSHIRE

Before I was ordained to the diaconate in April 2002, my ministry focused on youth. I worked as a co-leader of an ecumenical youth group, and I tried to organize an area youth center in an attempt to offer an alternative to drugs and alcohol for the area youth. Almost immediately after my ordination, my wife left her cure as the rector of a church in rural Maine. After about six months, she accepted a call to a church in southern New Hampshire. I was concerned, having heard New Hampshire did not welcome diaconal ministry. I wondered what God had in mind for me. I was pleasantly surprised to be warmly welcomed by the bishop, who asked at our first meeting if I would serve as deacon at that morning's staff Eucharist.

Our new home, a high-growth area within commuting distance of Boston, is a very different environment than where I had served in Maine, with very different ministry needs. Once again I was in the process of discernment. When Bishop Douglas Theuner asked me what ministries I might do in New Hampshire, I replied that I was trying to discern God's will, but at the time I believed my ministry might be with the elderly and in prisons. The bishop assigned me to the diocese's prison concerns committee and began sending me around to several churches in the area. When asked which one might be a fit, I replied, "Bishop, all the churches you sent me to were large multi-staff churches. Are there any small churches where the priest might need some help?" Two days later the bishop called and asked me to go the next Sunday to Faith Church in Merrimack. I walked in the door and knew I was home. Faith Church is a family-size church with friendly, talented people who are welcoming and inclusive. Their joyful worship incorporates original music and innovative liturgy. Within a short period, I was assigned to Faith Church.

At the same time I was also beginning to look for work. We had been in New Hampshire for several months and my energies had been divided between church and settling into a new home. Just as circumstances were encouraging me to start looking for work, the diocese announced a position as pastoral excellence coordinator. Although the position description looked interesting, I did not know if a deacon would be considered since the primary work of the position was to be ministry development, not what I previously thought of as diaconal ministry. Within a week two priests told me I should apply for this position because "it was me," calling for a combination of my skills developed as an Air Force program manager and my diaconal gifts. I decided maybe I should listen to my colleagues and to God, and applied for the position, giving prayerful attention to how this combination might apply to the position. I was excited when I received the call for an interview, and when the bishop asked me, "Do you think this is a deacon's work?" I

✳

replied, "Yes, Bishop, it is the work of deacons, it is the work of priests, it is the work of bishops, and it is the work of lay people."

When I received the bishop's call offering me the pastoral excellence coordinator's position, I realized that the ministry God was calling me to at this time and in this place was ministry development, the calling of all people into ministry. One of my main objectives is to develop baptismal enrichment teams. The teams form a covenant group and enter into discernment, trying to understand what ministries their parishes are called to do and who has been given the gifts to accomplish these ministries. Our ultimate goal is to empower all people to respond to God's call to ministry of one form or another.

## KEITH MCCOY, DIOCESE OF NEW JERSEY

As I was finishing college, a few parishioners suggested that I should go to seminary and be a "minister" (this was in low church Massachusetts in the early 1970s). I enjoyed being of service, but could not see myself in the priest's role. That, and struggles with my sexuality, convinced me not to pursue that course.

Flash forward a few years. I completed a master's in library science, took up residence in New Jersey, came out of the closet, found a church home, got involved. A parishioner at Christ Church was ordained to the diaconate, not to be a priest, but to be a deacon. Her name was Carol Kerbel, and she wasn't shy about promoting this ministry of service. That idea interested me. So when the Diocese of New Jersey announced that they would have an experimental program to train deacons, I went to Carol and told her I was interested. She said that it was good that I had come to her, because she was planning to come get me. Four years later, in 1985, I was ordained as part of the first class of deacons in the diocese, and as its first openly gay cleric.

Early on, before and after ordination, I did youth work. The kids were fine with my being gay (not that I beat people over the head with my sexual orientation), but it made a few diocesan officials nervous, and a few parents objected, even to the point of concocting rumors. After thirteen years of that ministry in two parishes, I felt exhausted. The average tenure of a church youth worker is eighteen months, so I was skewing the statistics by doing this for so long. The new rector at my second parish said he wanted to do youth work, so I gladly stepped aside. I spent several nervous months wondering, "What will I do next?" Eventually, I found myself in the office of Bishop Coadjutor Joe Morris Doss, along with two other deacons. Joe wanted to revive the diaconate program in the diocese in a big way (it had been dormant for almost five years at this point), and I ended up as the chair of a fledgling committee.

For eight years, the creation of new deacons was my ministry. We spun off from the committee the archdeacon's role, and a council for existing deacons. I got involved with NAAD and chaired some committees that studied and rethought the educational needs of deacons. Bishop Doss gave me a free hand and some funding, and we produced three classes of deacons, and started a fourth.

Bishop Doss left New Jersey under strained circumstances in 1999. An interim bishop came in and wanted to be more hands-on than I liked to work under, so I resigned to give him an opportunity to select the leadership he wanted. Just before this, I resigned from my second parish after thirteen years of service. It had been a busy time but draining, and I knew I needed time off. This time around, I was more at ease with God, and I decided I would be still and wait for God to tell me what was next.

I church shopped for almost a year, and enjoyed the feeling of just sitting in a pew, watching and listening, singing and praying. I eventually joined another parish, and two years later, I am still delighted to be there. Due to professional demands (I am running a third small library, and serve as treasurer of the New Jersey Library Association) and some personal changes (such as splitting up and moving away from my partner of seventeen years), I am too far from my parish to be of much assistance except on Sundays, but I do keep my ears and eyes open for the rector, make sure he takes time off, and let him ventilate occasionally without it going any further.

My new ministry came about after a couple of gay and lesbian clergy colleagues came to me for advice about issues relating to partner benefits, deployment, and the election of a new bishop. It seemed to me that here was a group that needed some direction to meet its own needs. So, I have become the organizer and convener of the diocesan gay/lesbian clergy—all twenty-nine of us. We have developed an agenda of issues that affect us, from spiritual health to parish survival, and we are about to start working on possible solutions.

✳

As I look back on thirty-five years of working in libraries and eighteen years of ordained service to the church, I see that I have developed a ministry of organization. I continually end up in situations where systems have broken down, or don't even exist. I bring people together, get them to think through issues to develop a plan of action, and then walk with them down that new path. Even my preaching tends towards getting people to hear the familiar in a new way.

After I was ordained, the friend who preached at my celebration of a new ministry compared deacons to sheepdogs (he owned one, so he knew what he was talking about). I prefer to think of myself as a corgi, but the imagery is the same: nipping at heels, rounding up the flock, and heading them in the direction they need to go. I have at least twenty more years of service ahead of me. I figure God will let me know what's next on the list when the right time comes.

## LORRAINE MILLS-CURRAN, DIOCESE OF RHODE ISLAND (LICENSED IN MASSACHUSETTS)

I am called to be present in Christ with kids. I have had additional calls: I was already a lawyer when I was ordained, and I have a wonderful marriage with three children. But this call is central and the one to which I always return. I think it is based in my own youthful frustration with the church. I was very serious about faith at a young age but could not get the church to take me very seriously.

I have lived out this call in my diaconate in various ways. Already active in youth ministry at every level from local to national, I was ordained fifteen years ago in Rio Grande. Spiritual development in young people seems to occur almost entirely as a result of "contagion," so I looked for every venue in which such contagion could occur.

After a move to Rhode Island, I continued my youth ministry, primarily at the deanery level. I also served for three years as the diocesan parish youth ministry coordinator. I brought my diaconate into my paid work life by shifting my law career from the Small Business Administration into legal advocacy work for children with disabilities. But this shift was problematic, since I was a federally paid employee. It really was not appropriate to bring spirituality into that workplace.

I entered seminary in 1997, trying to reshape my ministry life so it did not feel so scattered. My seminary experience started peculiarly: I was not admitted to the local Episcopal seminary because my vocation was "unclear." I still think they did not know then what a diaconal vocation was. But it turned out for the best, because I ended up at Weston Jesuit School of Theology. The Jesuits gave me generous financial support out of the goodness of their hearts, and I will always be grateful.

Attending a Roman Catholic seminary as an ordained woman was a unique experience. I mined the tradition for tools to help the kids I loved. I also learned a great deal about the difficult task of ecumenism. I am putting these insights to work as a newly appointed member of the Standing Commission on Ecumenism and Interreligious Relations, and have recently entered into the ongoing ecumenical dialogue concerning diaconal theology. I represented the Episcopal Church at the International Center for the Diaconate's theological symposium in Stuttgart, Germany, in November 2003.

I have worked for the last few years at St. Paul's Episcopal Church in Natick, Massachusetts, where I supervise the Christian formation of about 180 children and youth. I have a dream job in a booming parish; it feels like the 1960s here.

My newest focus is investigating possibilities for bringing effective religious education to local deaf children, who are currently underserved. This is an expensive and complicated process for a parish to undertake. But it will be possible, with God's help and the help of a church community that seems to find no limits in its dedication to children. I hope this ministry will be the next step in making sure that the faith of every child that comes my way gets taken seriously, all for the greater glory of God.

### DUTTON MOREHOUSE, DIOCESE OF FOND DU LAC

For a couple of years I was the chaplain for the neurosurgery unit of Children's Hospital of Michigan. We had a number of brain-injured kids we called our "frequent fliers," who were in and out of the hospital with unfortunate regularity. Needless to say, the kids, and perhaps to a greater extent their mothers and grandmothers, became an extended family to which I was privileged to minister as friend and spiritual supporter.

As a professional chaplain, it was pretty clear that I was simply a conduit for the healing grace of Jesus Christ and not the healer myself. The power of this agency function was brought home to me with considerable force through the events of one afternoon. It was not a special afternoon. I remember being in a room with the usual two patients and quite an assortment of family and friends of both. I honestly had no recollection of what was said that afternoon—just that it was a friendly, wide-ranging discussion that was not especially religious in content.

A couple of weeks later, one of the mothers who had been in that room came to me and asked if I remembered that afternoon and specifically one young man who had been there. I said yes, vaguely. "Well," she said, "you saved his life that afternoon." Of course this was impossible, and I expressed my doubts. "It's true," she persisted. "He told me later that he had just come to grips with the fact that he is gay, and he had decided to kill himself because he couldn't face his family. He said that what you said in that room changed his mind, and he decided he could go on with life."

I still have no idea what I said . . . what could possibly have meant enough to him that he would decide against suicide. Clearly it wasn't me, it was the healing power of Christ. It's a mystery.

## PAM NESBIT, DIOCESE OF PENNSYLVANIA

In April 2002 fourteen members of St. Andrew's Episcopal Church in Yardley, Pennsylvania, with a little help from our friends, were the Anglican church on Caye Caulker, Belize. Officially, there is no Anglican church on Caye Caulker. There is a small Roman Catholic church and a very enthusiastic Assembly of God church, but there is no building, as yet, for Anglican worship.

The fourteen of us who went down to Belize were working as part of a joint project of Episcopal Relief and Development and the Anglican Diocese of Belize to help build sturdy, low-cost housing on the island of Caye Caulker, which was devastated by Hurricane Keith in September 2000. The day the first group arrived, the cinder-block walls on the house we were to work on were about four feet high. When the first group left, they were up to the roof sill. When the second group left, the walls were finished, the roof beams were in place, and the septic tank was dug. The house was ready for occupation soon after.

The house we were building was to be purchased by a woman named Alejandra. She is a Belizean woman from the mainland, orphaned as a child, who came to Caye Caulker years ago when she married a man from the island. She and her husband were not able to have children, and he divorced her years ago. She is now alone and handicapped from complications of diabetes, unable to move around well enough to bake the bread that she used to sell. Her nephew is helping her buy the house so she can have indoor plumbing and enough room for someone to stay with her.

I sat with Ali in her termite-ridden shack next to the building site and heard her story. She has felt alone and rejected all her life. Her background is Roman Catholic, and she is sad and bitter that the local church has not helped her. She told me she was rejected even by the church. I pointed out the window at the grubby St. Andrew's parishioners who were mixing mortar and building walls and said, "Ali, look out your window. There is the church, come to build you a house."

Dusty, sweaty, dedicated, tired, patient, generous, laughing, harried people—praying together, working together to build a house, looking out for each other. That was the Anglican Church on Caye Caulker.

### DAPHNE B. NOYES, DIOCESE OF MASSACHUSETTS

[From a report to her congregation:] Many of you know me as a Sunday morning person—someone who is here for the liturgy regularly, preaches occasionally, grabs a quick bite at coffee hour sometimes, attends vestry meetings usually. As accurate as this is, it covers less than one-seventh of my time. So my report today is a "diaconate 101" if you will—a quick survey of my activities over the past year or so.

But first, by way of background, I want to talk a bit about the deacon's function and identity, and how those two aspects are blended in ways that present both challenge and opportunity to the deacon (and here I use third person since this is true for most deacons), as well as to the congregation and the church itself. Probably the entry point for understanding this is to note that unlike most parish clergy, I do not earn my living through the work I do for the church. A deacon's ministry is non-stipendiary—church-talk for unpaid. This does not make me a volunteer, per se, since as an ordained person there is never a time when I am not a deacon. My

145

diaconal service is not confined to the Sunday morning liturgy, or the time I spend ministering to patients, families, and staff at Massachusetts General Hospital. A deacon is always a deacon—that's the identity piece—no matter what the deacon is doing—the function piece.

You know that I have been assigned by the bishop to serve at this parish. That's primarily the functional part—the part that entails proclaiming the gospel, preaching, dismissing, and otherwise participating and assisting at the liturgy. But my service to the church—and to this parish—does not begin when I walk in the door Sunday morning, any more than it ends when I walk out the door a few hours later.

Like many of you, I take part in a range of "churchy" activities outside this parish. In the past year, I served as a member of Gayle Harris's ordination and consecration committee. With a number of people experienced in emergency preparedness, I was a member of a group that planned and coordinated a training session in this area at a September workshop at the cathedral. For a number of years, I've been involved with the Assembly of Episcopal Healthcare Chaplains (AEHC), an organization of American and Canadian chaplains working in hospitals, long-term care facilities, nursing homes, and VA hospitals.

Closer to home, as I enter into my tenth year as a volunteer chaplain at the Massachusetts General Hospital, I've been gratified by the development of two new partnerships in this area. The first, with the clergy of the Church of the Advent, means that a service of Holy Eucharist is now offered weekly in the hospital's beautiful chapel, a tranquil oasis instituted by our own Bishop Lawrence in the 1930s. The second, with Episcopal Church Women, will provide additional support for this work.

Many of you know there's a handful—a growing handful—of deacons in this diocese. I've been instrumental in arranging informal, occasional gatherings of this group, and have also worked with the Society of St. John the Evangelist to offer annual retreats for deacons; thus far, we have had deacons from New York, Chicago, Texas, Connecticut, and Massachusetts.

But my service to the church—and to this parish—is not restricted to these easily identifiable churchy activities. Like many of you, I earn my living in a determinedly secular organization—in my case, WGBH, the public television station, where I serve as senior publicist for American Experience, the historical documentary series. It can be a challenge to be intentional about my diaconate at my day job—just as I suspect many of you are challenged to live out your baptismal vows at the places where you work. The pressures of constant deadlines, personality conflicts, ethical quandaries, high expectations, and low budgets don't serve to bring out the best in people. But at work I am conscious of the world's hunger for meaning, and for mercy, and I do my best to walk with my colleagues and offer a presence that is sometimes supportive, sometimes challenging, but always thoughtful and prayerful.

### RODGER PATIENCE, DIOCESE OF MILWAUKEE

As the son and grandson of Episcopal priests, and the godson of an Episcopal bishop, I often joke that I "didn't stand a chance." Though I followed my namesakes into the ordained ministry, I found in the diaconate the life to which God was calling me. The constant challenge of translation—crossing borders between the church and the world, between lay and ordained, between young and old—is what invigorates me and keeps my ministry fresh.

My wife, Katrin, and I live in southern Wisconsin. She is a high school English teacher in Williams Bay, and I commute five hours each day to downtown Chicago, where I am a member of the clinical information systems team at Northwestern Memorial Hospital. I support the software needs of Prentice Women's Hospital as well as the bed tracking software used throughout the three pavilions of the 750-bed healthcare facility.

I see my daily work as diaconal: Whenever someone comes to me in a panic because their computer is not working, my first words are the gospel message of the angels—"don't be afraid." My role in the hospital—just like in the church—is not necessarily to provide front-line care, but to support and enable those who do.

In the church, my main ministry is to present workshops on the prevention of child abuse and sexual misconduct, work I have done ever since the Church Insurance Company began mandating such training more than a decade ago. I have trained several hundred people in the dioceses of Chicago and Milwaukee, and I have consulted with parishes and other Midwestern dioceses on the creation of their own training programs. I have also served on a team responding to allegations of sexual abuse in parishes.

147

✳

In the Diocese of Milwaukee, I serve as a member of the Deacon Formation Committee and have played a major role in the design of the School for Deacons. I teach prayer book theology, liturgics, and homiletics.

As one of the less than one percent of Episcopal deacons under the age of forty, I am also active in initiatives that encourage young vocations. I am a member of "Gathering the Next Generation" (GTNG), the national network of GenX Episcopalians (born 1961–1981) and one of a team of young clergy and lay people who created "Hearing the Still, Small Voice," a vocations retreat offered each year in Province V. Through GTNG's email groups, I also exercise a ministry of diaconal presence and teaching.

One of the earliest photographs in our family's albums shows me at the age of two with my father's stole around my neck and his prayer book in my lap. Though I felt called to ordained ministry from an early age, there were very few deacons from whom I could learn about their ministry. I hope, in part, to show others that the diaconate is a ministry for young adults who can "fulfill their vows to the Lord in the presence of all his people."

## KAY SALINARO, DIOCESE OF CALIFORNIA

I was ordained in December 1985. Prior to then, I had been involved in numerous ministries, most of which have continued through the years. In the 1970s I became involved with a friend in beginning a ministry to residents in convalescent homes, working with administrators to match volunteers, one to one, with residents who had no family or friends visiting them. We formed a board with leaders from the community, recruited volunteers from all denominations and faiths, and provided them with training. Some years later my friend died, and I retired from the board, remaining on the advisory board. This ministry spread throughout Contra Costa and Alameda counties in the Bay Area and is still going strong. I continued a leadership role in convalescent ministry until 1999, sometimes working with Deacon Arlinda Cosby.

For a number of years I worked in hospital administration. For twenty years (1978–1997) I was employed at a Medical/Education Center for the Developmentally Disabled, which served disabled persons from birth to death.

It was my involvement in these ministries that caused my rector to suggest that I become a deacon. This was in the late 1970s when most of us didn't have much idea of what a "deacon" was. Bishop William Swing had arrived in the Diocese of California, and the School for Deacons was being formed under the direction of the Very Rev. Shirley Woods. Through prayer, and urging by my rector, along with much support from others, I enrolled in this new school, in the first class. By this time, I was also involved in jail ministry through "Friends Outside," a Quaker group. After ordination, I became a spiritual advisor for Kairos in the local federal prison for women and worked Cursillo weekends.

In college I majored in music, sang professionally in the San Francisco Opera Company, the San Francisco Symphony Chorus, light opera productions, and choral groups, and gave recitals. In 1984 I was assigned to a mission where I served for fifteen years, helping them develop an adult choir, a youth choir, and various other music programs. This mission has developed a good understanding of the role of the deacon and has been very supportive of deacons through the years. They have sponsored three deacons.

I began teaching various subjects at the School for Deacons in 1987, including liturgical practicum, music for deacons: chanting the gospel, the Exsultet, the liturgy for Palm Sunday, Holy Week, and the Easter Vigil. The bishop assigned me to the school as their deacon, and I continue in this ministry.

In 2000 the bishop assigned me to La Santisima Trinidad Mission, a Spanish-speaking congregation. He sent me to Mexico for three weeks where I attended a Spanish language school and lived with a Mexican family. It was a wonderful experience. I continue to learn Spanish and the Latino culture in order to best serve them.

I have served on numerous diocesan commissions. As a member of companion relationship with the Episcopal Church in Jerusalem and the Middle East, I was sent to Israel during the 1988 intifada to assist in developing an education curriculum to help us learn about each other. I now serve on the commission on ministry; world mission commission, which supports local parishes in various world ministries throughout the world; and the peace, justice, and hunger commission, which supports these ministries in the diocese. I was elected the first alternate clergy deputy to General Convention. I was also privileged to serve the North American Association for the Diaconate as its president (2000–2002), which afforded me opportunities to travel worldwide, learning about deacons and the diaconate in the world.

I have seen much change in the diaconate in the past twenty years, and have been very blessed to be a part of that change. I am sure the deacon's role will continue to evolve as more deacons are ordained, and the church realizes its call to model Christ's servant ministry in the church and the world.

## Marcia Stackhouse, Diocese of Colorado

I was ordained June 29, 1988, but the journey started at least fifteen years earlier when I had a vivid dream that God was calling me to be a deacon. At that time, women were not allowed to be ordained, and I had never even seen or read about deacons. What I did think I knew was that deacons were ordained old men who visited people in the hospital, and that it was necessary to complete seminary to be ordained. At that time I had not even finished college and had three young children. How could I possibly finish college now, move to Nashotah (the only seminary I knew of), and finish seminary? And were there any tall buildings in Nashotah (my husband was an elevator constructor)? The barriers seemed too high, so I decided I was having delusions of grandeur due to my growing relationship with God, Jesus, and the Holy Spirit. That denial worked for about ten years as we continued to raise our children and grow in our relationship with God and the church.

When the call to the diaconate came strongly in 1983, I had the courage to speak to our priest and to make an appointment with the woman who was organizing the first class of people called to the diaconate. I started my journey toward ordination, a journey of five more years. During the first four years of preparation the vestry of the church wanted me to be a "pastoral assistant," working with the poor, mentally ill, and elderly members of the congregation, so I aimed my formation toward that goal. During the last year, the vestry decided to hire a youth minister instead. I was glad that I had also aimed my education to be able to do social work in the private or public sector.

Immediately after ordination, I was hired as a social caseworker by a non-profit agency that housed the homeless, a ministry I did for four years. Prior to ordination, I had worked for the Episcopal Pastoral Center, an emergency assistance agency in the Denver inner city. Working with the homeless seemed to be a natural for me. When the funding for that job ended, I was hired by the Department of Social Services as a child protection worker, a ministry I continue to do. Working with families is one of my passions.

I am serving in my fourth church since ordination. The first was a medium-sized church with a varied population, the second was a Lutheran-Episcopal church, the third was a pastoral church becoming a program church, and the current is a small inner-city church. In each of these churches I have been involved in outreach to the community. I have assisted at Sunday and some weekday services, and done occasional funerals and weddings. At two of these churches I have been involved in the worship committee and parish council. As an outgrowth of my child protection job, I also teach parenting classes and child abuse prevention classes in the diocese. I have overseen eucharistic ministers and occasionally take communion to the hospitalized and homebound.

I am fascinated with Central America and have visited three countries there. My ongoing love is Guatemala, and I have been there eight times, three times leading mission teams. I have an ongoing struggle to become more fluent in Spanish to communicate with the people more easily. My husband and I have sponsored three children, one in El Salvador and two in Guatemala. It is a joy to meet these children and their families and to be in third world countries where a little help can make a difference in the lives of some of the people.

I cannot forget to mention the support systems that sustain me. I attend clergy conferences, conventions, and retreats, have a spiritual director, and have been a member of the same clergy wellness group for twelve years. We meet twice a month for two hours and have a trained facilitator for our group. These are my most trusted colleagues with whom I am able to share the struggles of my personal, professional, and diaconal life. We have prayed and walked through many crises in each of our lives. I am also a weaver and a knitter, crafts that help me live out my creativity.

## GERI SWANSON, DIOCESE OF NEW YORK

It was the very first night I spent doing my clinical pastoral piece for formation. I was working form 3:00 p.m. until 11:00 p.m. at a local nursing home. I had sat through several hours of orientation about how to proceed, the protocol of the facility, and what was

151

expected of me in my role has chaplain for the seventh and eighth floors.

I met with the evening nurses and other staff, introduced myself to the list of Episcopalians and other mainline folk who would be my responsibility for the next six months, and then slumped into an empty chair in a darkened and vacant room. I gazed out over the trees of the property and looked to the Atlantic Ocean that spread out before me and began to pray: "Lord, what am I doing here? What is your plan for me here? Can I ever achieve anything in this place?" I sat in the darkness for what seemed an eternity—actually about twenty minutes—and then got up to make my final round. I stopped outside the door where I heard a woman quietly weeping. I washed my hands and went inside.

She was about eighty years old. The nurse had told me she was the widow of a local pastor, and she would be undergoing surgery the next day. I stood at her side and touched her trembling hand. She turned to me and asked if I would pray with her. I began the Lord's Prayer, and she joined in Spanish. I then recited a prayer from compline: "Keep watch, dear Lord, with those who work or watch or weep this night." She began to breathe easier, she closed her eyes—"and give your angels charge over those who sleep." Her eyelids grew heavier and heavier, but she held tightly to my hand—"give rest to the weary . . . soothe the suffering . . . shield the joyous." She was finally asleep—"and all for your love's sake. Amen." I left the room knowing why I had been sent there.

The next week I was there, the night nurse told me that the woman insisted to her daughter that an angel—*angeli*—had visited her in the night to help get her ready for her operation. Angelic messenger? Deacon? What an awe-filled responsibility we take upon ourselves when we say "yes" to the call!

## JIM UPTON, DIOCESE OF KANSAS

In the years since I was ordained, I have learned a lot about what it means to be a deacon, some of it even right. But I learned one of my greatest lessons when I became a representative payee for a mentally ill man.

Aunt Wanda came looking for help for Chuck. Chuck was a forty-year-old man who had been identified as manic-depressive in his early thirties. His mental illness had cost him his marriage, his job, and, aside from Aunt Wanda, his family. Dealing with Chuck

152

and his money was becoming too difficult for her, and since she was a member of the church she came to me to see if someone might become Chuck's representative payee for his Social Security disability money. Little did I know that working with Chuck would change my understanding of ministry and my understanding of myself as a deacon.

Becoming Chuck's representative payee was easily done; the Social Security Administration just transferred his case to me, and the bill paying and expense money allocations were pretty simple. But Chuck's illness was anything but simple. His wild highs and deep depressions took him in and out of the state hospital, various psych wards, treatment centers, group homes, and jail. There were times when his request to handle his own money was granted and he tried to live his life as normally as possible. But his "living normally" meant not taking his medication, and the symptoms of his mental illness always came back with a vengeance; in depression he attempted suicide several times, in manic phases, he was everywhere, running at life twenty-four hours a day. Soon Chuck was again deeply in debt, usually back in an emergency treatment center or in jail, evicted from his rooms, all that he had accumulated lost to the street or sheriff's sale.

I quickly found there wasn't any fixing for Chuck; his illness wasn't going to go away. A little more money or discipline or effort wasn't going to make things right. All I could do was to stay connected, walk with him through the good and bad times, and share with him my faith that in the end all will be well. Chuck likes to remind me that he "is no Christian," and it took me years to know my answer to him: "I know Chuck, but I am."

Being Chuck's payee is an important task, but my ministry with Chuck is to stay connected with him, through his ups and downs, through hospital and jail time, and back in the community, and to help him stay connected to the world around him. Not because this will fix him, but because beyond the illness and the bad choices Chuck is a man loved by God, and for some reason God has put us on the path together. Is this ministry out in the world, is this pastoral care, or is this worshiping? I don't know, and I don't think it matters.

What I have learned is that I can help Chuck remember who he is by helping him stay connected with the world around him, by reminding him that he is a valued and loved part of creation, and

153

✳

that there are people and places that need him. What I have learned in the years being Chuck's payee is that the need to stay connected, to be reminded of our value, to need and be needed, is important to us all. This has changed my understanding of ministry and my understanding of who I am.

An important part of my ministry as a deacon has become simply to help—help find the connections and to stay connected, help uncover the value that is already there, help people discern their needs and how and where they are needed, and help them find their connections to God and to one another, to feel their value as part of God's creation.

## JOHN WILLETS, DIOCESE OF CHICAGO

As I reflect on the past ten plus years since my ordination, I begin to think about the possibilities I've had that couldn't have been anticipated. Being ordained in the Diocese of Los Angeles, I was privileged to attend Bishop Chester Talton on many episcopal visits throughout that diocese. I think back on those experiences now and realize what a cross-section of the church I was exposed to. With all the richness in socioeconomic and cultural diversity, I was exposed to a vision of the church in Los Angeles that many people never experience. This was both instructional but more important formational in my own spiritual life and work as a deacon.

Very early on, I began to understand that how I framed the questions to those I met along the way would affect my formation in ministry. As an example, during my preordination years I was asked by folks over and over, "What will you be able to do as an ordained person you can't do now?" The question always seemed too personally focused, too limited in scope. The real question was, "What will the church be able to do when you're ordained that it can't do now?"

I've come to think of all ministry as shaped by our baptismal covenant. In that regard, it seems that the last three promises of the covenant are particularly relevant to the diaconal ministry. As a deacon my responsibility is shaped by these questions, and my ministry is to assist in the development of all the baptized, helping and equipping all to grow into diaconal ministry. As an animator of diaconal gifts, my task is to do diaconal ministry as a member of the church by baptism, but as an ordained deacon my task is to assist the church in the development of diaconal ministry of all the baptized.

Taking on this vision, I have come to think of churchgoers as church-going-insiders and gospel-carrying-outsiders. We need to live into both these roles. The former seems especially well developed in the church and presbyteral. The latter seems to require particular attention and diaconal. As animator of diaconal ministry, I've changed the dismissal at Calvary to: "Go into the world carrying the gospel of Christ." As animator and developer of diaconal ministry, my accountability to my congregation is to assist, identify, and develop diaconal possibilities in myself and others.

CHAPTER NINE

✳

# PASCHAL DEACONS IN A PASCHAL CHURCH

O nce upon a time, a theater company in a small town performed Shakespeare's *Romeo and Juliet* every spring. As is
common in rural communities, everybody pitched in and
had a role to play. Some performed major parts, some bit parts.
Some made costumes, some built scenery, and some sold tickets.
Some just came and applauded. Everyone had a good time and
enjoyed the play.

Then tragedy struck! The man and woman who played the title
roles took their characters too seriously and ran off together. The
town was shocked. What to do about the play? Finally one of the
bit actors, a woman of robust conceit, offered to play both Romeo
and Juliet. At every performance she changed from tights to gown,
and back, from tenor to soprano ("O Romeo, Romeo! wherefore art
thou, Romeo?"), and back, and rushed from side to side, from balcony to garden, from one line to the next. Everybody else was
stunned into silence, but if anyone found her behavior bizarre, no
one said so.

By and by the company appointed a new director, with democratic tendencies, who resolved the controversy. Every actor
received every possible chance to play every character in every
scene. One played Romeo in the balcony scene, another in the duel
scene, another in the death scene. As for Juliet, every man, woman,
and child wanted to play her, and most of them did—at each per-

formance. Everybody else was stunned into silence, but if anyone found this confusion bizarre, no one said so.

Finally, the oldest person in the town remembered how things had been in the old days, before all the fuss and change. With a new director and a much-relieved cast, the company settled down and performed the play the old way, one person to each role. Everybody was delighted with this orderly participation, and everybody said so.[1]

When deacons tell their stories, they talk about their congregations, their bishop, those within and those without, and the roles all play. In their stories we see the totality of the diaconate. In a multitude of ways, many servants, many agents of the church, carry out ministry by action, word, and personal attendance. The diaconate finds manifestation, and meaning finds expression, not in any one deacon but in the entire community of deacons in each diocese, and in all the deacons of the holy catholic church, interacting with each other and with others.

The stories of deacons reveal two principal themes: first, the importance of *agape* in their life and work, and second, their growing sense that they are *diakonoi* or agents of someone or some group, maybe the bishop, maybe the church, maybe the poor and oppressed, maybe all these. Not all deacons have made up their minds about who they are and what they do, and exploration and surprise remain traits of an evolving order.

## THE IMPORTANCE OF *AGAPE*

Much of the appeal of the diaconate, much of the happy face it turns to the world, flows from the activity of *agape*, which is sometimes called charity (from the Latin *caritas*) or, better, divine love. The love of God for all creation leads all human beings to love God and one another, and those who do not love, through hatred or cold indifference, fail deeply their basic human nature, their imbedded image of God. Deacons in our time are symbols and energizers of this divinely inspired outpouring.

As set forth in Scripture, however, divine love has nothing directly to do with the order of deacons. It is not one of the diaconal qualifications listed in 1 Timothy 3. It is, instead, an obligation for all. All who wish to inherit eternal life must love God and one another. To illustrate the second part of the requirement, Jesus tells the parable of the Good Samaritan, in Luke 10:29–37. The Samaritan shows mercy on the victim of a robbery, gives him first aid and shelter, and cares for him. The Samaritan is not a Jew, not a Christian, not a deacon. He is a righteous one.

Christ's exhortation to merciful activity in Matthew 25:31–44 is often cited as a guide for diaconal activity. Again, this passage has nothing to do with deacons. It sets forth an obligation for all. All are to feed the hungry, give drink to the thirsty, welcome the stranger, clothe the naked, care for the sick, and visit those in prison. Often overlooked in the midst of good works is the setting, Judgment Day. The righteous who observe these good deeds will inherit eternal life; the unrighteous who neglect them will merit eternal punishment.

It's a sugar and switch approach to behavior, and it works. The fundamental goodness of human nature works. Christ attracts those who listen. For in every age, in a climate of violence and fear and greed and oppression, Christians of many kinds have sought and served Christ in others, have striven for justice and peace, have respected the dignity of human nature. Mother Teresa of Calcutta is not unique, or even rare, in the history of Christian people, or of the human race.

From the beginning, the church has assigned deacons a special place in the execution of *agape*, but this place has more to do with the nature of the church than with the nature of deacons. When Laurence pointed to the sick and poor of Rome as "the treasures of the church," he was speaking about a major concern of the Christian community. The assembly and its members took care of those in need—among themselves, in other churches, and in the city around them. Mercy was their communal and personal duty. As a major church official, the "prime minister" (which is what *archidiakonos* really means), Laurence assisted the bishop by overseeing the distribution of charity. Some of the other deacons (ministers of state) oversaw and performed good works in special areas, such as running cemeteries, and subdeacons (assistant ministers of state) helped them with numerous details. This was how the church functioned to carry out its crucial mission of divine love.

Today the church functions differently. For good or ill, order is not as important as it once was in the arrangement of household duties. In our culture we incline toward the casual and democratic.

159
✳

Ancient tradition, however, remains a strong source of motivation in the way we order our ministry. The preface to the ordination rites states clearly: "It is also a special responsibility of deacons to minister in Christ's name to the poor, the sick, the suffering, and the helpless." When the bishop tells the ordinands that their "life and teaching are to show Christ's people that in serving the helpless they are serving Christ himself," this exhortation does not mean that deacons are to become "righteous ones" as a special condition of ordination. Like the Jew, the Christian is expected to be righteous from the start. The special duty of deacons is to show the way to righteousness—the way in which God's people learn to love mercy and do justice. There are two main paths in which deacons show the way:

First, deacons are *icons* of righteousness. Although the word *icon* has become grossly overused—to stand for almost everything from rock stars to gewgaws on a computer screen—it retains theological value in the Christian tradition. By looking at deacons, and following them in ministry, Christian people are able to reach beyond the surface appearance and participate in activities of the kingdom. Deacons are outward and visible signs of the presence of Christ in the poor, and of our response to his presence. As signs they possess within themselves the quality of life they attempt to portray. The icon, the sign, draws us within itself.

Second, deacons are *leaders* of righteousness. They lead in several ways. They organize and administer works of mercy. More subtly, they tell stories, teach, and exhort the people to mercy. They stir the pot. Where I live, in south Louisiana, we make a basic sauce called roux out of flour and oil. You must stir the pot continuously, or the sauce will burn. So it is with deacons and the Christian community; deacons stir up the people so they won't burn.

## A SENSE OF *DIAKONIA*

If you want to find out whom deacons call boss, look at the ordination rite: "God now calls you to a special ministry directly under your bishop." Subordination to the bishop is not involuntary servility or slavery. It is agency, service carried out with urgency and high purpose. A *diakonos* is one who acts for another, who is the voice of the other's will, who executes the other's desires through forceful word, swift action, and devoted attendance. Consequently, *diakonia* is the activity of being an agent. As the ancient folk-etymology had it, *diakonia* means "through the dust," and *diakonos* is one who raises the dust. In a whirlwind of activity, *diakonos* and the other are one in mind, heart, and spirit.

Deacons in the Episcopal Church serve (that is, act) "directly" under the bishop. The juxtaposition of deacons and bishop implies personal contact and harmony of purpose. (Deacons in the Anglican Church of Canada serve "directly under the authority" of the bishop, although in reality their relationship is not as remote and abstract as the liturgical phrase implies.) In the ancient church deacons were the "ministers" of the bishop, more like cabinet officers than household servants. They were his eyes and ears, and they spoke with his voice and authority. This was not just a noble theory; early deacons such as Laurence and Vincent suffered death because of their direct contact with the bishop and identification as his agents, his prime ministers and secretaries of state. Because they were ministers of the bishop, ordained to the bishop, they were agents of the local church, ordained to the mission of the church.



In an age when the diocese was the parish church, bishop and deacons lived in the same city, saw each other daily, and prayed and worked in intimacy. Today we have to be creative and invent personal contact where little exists. Some bishops have done a good job by meeting with their deacons, corresponding with them, attending their retreats and meetings, and taking deacons on visitations to congregations. The restoration of the classic archidiaconate in almost half our dioceses is another healthy sign of bishops acting through their deacons.

For bishop and deacons to be one, and to carry out the mission of the church with one heart, they must support each other. There must exist in the diocese a rare leader, truly an image of God the Father. We are fortunate in North America to have many bishops, men and women, who know how to act through their deacons. They take seriously the imperative at their own ordination to "guide and strengthen the deacons." Sadly, not all bishops want deacons, and a few deserve none.

Similarly, we need deacons who can work for bishops, discern their will, carry out their desires, and, yes, talk back to them and tell them the truth. I am not aware of any diocese that requires boldness in its diaconal candidates, or that teaches "Serving the

Bishop" in its formation program. A diocese without these qualifications of agency is missing the essence of the diaconate. Alongside gentleness and humility belong toughness and audacity. Wash the feet of the poor, indeed, but when you carry out activities for the bishop stir up the dust with your marching, your running, your dancing.

Deacons in a congregation also serve directly under their presbyter, and thus they are agents of the congregation, carrying out its will in whatever it desires. Ever since the fourth century, presbyters have functioned in congregations as de facto bishops (except for ordaining). In the practical life of the local church, the presbyter takes the bishop's place. Thus the relationship of presbyter and deacons resembles in almost every way that of bishop and deacons.

In carrying out the desires of the presbyter, deacons work with the presider, the president of the congregation, for the good of the congregation. Presbyter and deacon are colleagues, fellow workers, advisors, and companions. Wherever action is needed, deacons can step in and show the way. They are to take initiative and show enthusiasm, to lead where timid ones tremble, to charge where others hold back.

Why, then, do deacons not have a canonical place as officers in congregations? We have rectors and vicars, deans and canons, curates (by whatever name), and junior and senior wardens, but in most places deacons have no official title or status. If you want them, you can have them, but you don't have to have them. If you have them, you don't have to do anything with them, or to let them do anything. They are officers without office, deacons without deaconry, and their shaky place in congregations is a sign of a wobbly church.

This weakness is the church's loss, for the fundamental role of deacons is not to serve at the feet of bishops and presbyters but to act for the people of God. The purpose of an agent (or minister) is to enable everyone to participate actively in the life of the church. Deacons are agents of the church, that eternal gathering of those who love and serve the Lord. They exist within the community of the people of God, and they act for and with the community. Whatever they do, they never do alone. Always they represent both Christ and the church, helping the church to carry out its mission in the name of Christ. Even more significantly, they *present* Christ to the people of God that the people may *bear* Christ in the world.

As agents, deacons hold office and have a defined place in the life of the local church, especially in its liturgy. Their ministry is never theirs alone; it is Christ's, and it is the people's. They are accountable to the congregation, and the congregation is accountable to them for training and support. They bring the world to the congregation, and they bring the congregation to God's poor. They show the people the way of love, and the people carry out mercy and justice. They may be servants, but they are not servile. They are leaders called deacons.

Some years ago, at the ruins of Dachau concentration camp, a Roman Catholic deacon visited the site where horror once took place. Where cellblock 26 had stood he found a flower growing in the rubble. He picked the flower and pressed it between the pages of his Bible, a sign of life rising from the dust for those who walk through the dust.

Acting for God's people, announcing God's word, attending God's poor, deacons are paschal ministers in a paschal church. At the Great Vigil of Easter, after the people have followed the light of Christ into a darkened room, the deacon begins the Exsultet by calling on celestial angels, round earth, and mother church to rejoice in the victory of Christ. The imperative *exsultet* (from *ex* or "from" and *saltare* or "jump") means not only to rejoice, to feel a blissful emotion, but to leap up, repeatedly and even violently as in a wild dance.

I imagine the Exsultet as the deacon calling a boisterous square dance. The dancers—swarms of angels, the earth and all its inhabitants (the whole Noah's Ark entourage), and Mother Church (all the people of God, living and dead)—circle round and swing their partners. In cosmic steps the dancers recall the paschal lamb and praise God for the light of Christ. A square dance is energetic but not chaotic; the dancers rarely bump into each other or step on toes. It is orderly. The figures that all perform require precise execution, and the dancers listen carefully to the caller. This dance represents the order of creation brought to perfection through Christ. Exodus, crucifixion, and resurrection take place according to God's orderly plan.

And so this deacon ends in a familiar way, calling on God's people to perform their liturgical role in the paschal liturgy beyond place and time:

Dance now, angels, leap and fling,
grab a partner, circle round,
spirit hands who scrape the bow
fiddle a tune for Christ our king.

Enter, earth, and orbit right,
swing your corner, now your own,
astral lanterns dazzle dark,
round all fly in cosmic light.

Push back pew, complete the ring,
mother church in shimmy gown,
bring your loud and rowdy crowd,
fling this night for Christ our king.[2]

✳

APPENDIX A

✳

# Historic Documents

## A. Early ordination prayers

### Hippolytus, Apostolic Tradition (Rome, c. 215 or later)

God, who created all things and set them in order by the Word, Father of our Lord Jesus Christ, whom you sent to minister your will and to show us your desires, give the Holy Spirit of grace and care and diligence to this your servant, whom you have chosen to minister to your church and to offer [to bring forward] in your holy of holies the gifts offered you by your appointed high priests, so that serving without blame and with a pure heart, he may be counted worthy of this high office and glorify you through your Servant Jesus Christ, through whom glory and honor to you, the Father and the Son with the Holy Spirit in the holy church, both now and to the ages of ages.

### Apostolic Constitutions (Syria, late fourth century)

For men:

God the ruler of all, true and faithful, rich to all who call on you in truth, awesome in will, wise in mind, strong and great, hear our prayer, Lord, and listen to our plea, and show your face on this your slave, presented to you for the diaconate, and fill him with spirit and power, as you filled Stephen the martyr and imitator of the passion of your Christ, and make him fit to carry out the work of deacon committed to him, constant, blameless, and irreproachable, that he may be worthy of higher office, by the mediation of your only begotten Son, through whom in the Holy Spirit glory, honor, and veneration to you to the ages. Amen.

✳

For women:
God eternal, Father of our Lord Jesus Christ, creator of man and woman, who filled Miriam and Deborah and Hannah and Huldah with the Spirit, who did not shun the birth of your only begotten Son from a woman, and who in the tent of witness and in the temple set women as keepers of your holy doors, now look down on this your slave, presented for the diaconate, and give her your Holy Spirit, and cleanse her from all stain of flesh and spirit, that she may worthily complete the work committed to her, to your glory and the praise of your Christ, through whom in the Holy Spirit glory and worship to you to the ages. Amen.

## B. LAMBETH CONFERENCE AND ANGLICAN CONSULTATIVE COUNCIL

### Lambeth 1958: Resolution 88, "The Office of Deacon"

The Conference recommends that each province of the Anglican Communion shall consider whether the office of Deacon shall be restored to its primitive place as a distinctive order in the Church, instead of being regarded as a probationary period for the priesthood.

### Lambeth 1968: Resolution 32, "The Diaconate"

The Conference recommends:

(a) That the diaconate, combining service of others with liturgical functions, be open to (i) men and women remaining in secular occupations; (ii) full-time church workers; (iii) those selected for the priesthood.

(b) That Ordinals should, where necessary, be revised (i) to take account of the new role envisaged for the diaconate; (ii) by the removal of reference to the diaconate as "an inferior office"; (iii) by emphasis upon the continuing element of diakonia in the ministry of bishops and priests.

(c) That those made deaconesses by laying on of hands with appropriate prayers be declared to be within the diaconate.

(d) That appropriate canonical legislation be enacted by provinces and regional Churches to provide for those already ordained deaconesses.

## ACC-3 (1976): Conclusion of report on the diaconate

We appreciate Lambeth's concern to bring the serving or diaconal ministry of the Church more fully within the worshipping and liturgical functions of the whole community. We do not think that the making of deacons on a wider scale than hitherto would cause the laity to feel themselves to be released from responsibility to serve as well as to worship. We would therefore see the Diaconate conferred upon men and women who are deeply committed to Christ within the Church, and who are performing a caring and serving ministry in the world in the name of the Church, or who are carrying out a pastoral ministry in the Church.

## ACC-3 (1976): Resolution 10, "The Diaconate"

The Council advises:

(a) that the use of the Diaconate as a period of preparation for the priesthood be retained; and that every church should review its practice to ensure that this period is one of continued training and further testing of vocation; but that it is not to be regarded as necessarily leading to the priesthood;

(b) that the churches, and particularly the laity, be invited to examine the concept of the Diaconate as an Order to which lay people serving the Church, or serving in the name of the Church, could also be admitted, to express and convey the authority of the Church in their service. And, in this consideration, to take into account Resolution 32 of Lambeth 1968, and Bishop John Howe's article on the Diaconate written in preparation for that meeting of Lambeth. This study should include the status of deacons in Synods.

167

✳

## Lambeth Conference 1998: Study Document "Called to Be a Faithful Church in a Plural World"

### THE DIACONATE

87. In 1988, the Lambeth Conference noted that a number of developments were occurring in some of the churches of the Anglican Communion with regard to the diaconate as a separate and distinct order of ministry. These developments have continued since 1988, particularly in some of the churches of the northern hemisphere, and have also been considered ecumenically, especially in conversations with the Lutheran churches.

88. One of the significant issues raised by these developments is the identification of the ministry associated with the order of deacons. Like the ministries of oversight and priesthood, the ministry of service and proclamation of the word traditionally associated with the diaconate belongs to the whole laos. Where deacons exercise their special ministry within the Church, they do so by illuminating and holding up the servant ministry of the whole church and calling all its members to that ministry.

89. While all the churches of the Anglican Communion embrace servant-ministry as an integral part of their life together, not all have chosen to restore the diaconate to its more traditional form. In some places, specialised lay roles, such as the lay reader or catechist, may exercise similar functions on the local level.

90. Hence, renewed attention to the order of the diaconate also raises questions about its relationship to the church and the other orders with which its ministry is carried out. While deacons have traditionally been responsible directly to the bishop, the nature of their ministry often places them at the intersection between the church and the broader society in which they serve.

91. The last Lambeth Conference commended to the Provinces a review of member churches' ordinals and canons in order to identify and learn about the ministry of a distinctive and permanent diaconate. The 1998 Lambeth Conference provides the opportunity to carry on our reflection about the diaconal ministry in different contexts within the Anglican Communion and in the ecumenical context. How, in the varied settings represented within our Communion, can the relationship between servant-ministry and sacramental worship be clarified? How are we to understand the relationship between the ministry of deacons and priests as they serve to build up Christ's Body? How is the work of deacons on behalf of the church in the world drawn into and reflected in the life of the church and its member congregations?

✳

# CALENDAR OF DEACON SAINTS

This calendar of more than 200 deacons is assembled from several sources, including Anglican, Roman Catholic, Orthodox, and Lutheran calendars.

## JANUARY

3    Daniel, perhaps of Jewish descent, who aided the first bishop of Padua, martyred in northeast Italy, 168. (His body was discovered centuries later and solemnly enshrined 3 Jan. 1064.)

7    Clerus, martyred at Antioch in Syria, c. 300

8    Theophilus, martyred in Lybia, tortured and thrown into a furnace with the layman Helladius, ?

Dominika, abbess, Alexandria and Constantinople, 4th c.

Harriet Mary Bedell, missionary among the Seminoles and Mikosuki in Florida, 1969

10   Nicanor, one of the seven ordained by the apostles (Acts 6:5), according to tradition martyred in Cyprus, c. 76 [also July 28]

Theosebia, wife of Gregory of Nyssa, c. 387

12   Tatiana, martyred at Rome, c. 230

13   Hermylus, of Singidunum (Belgrade), martyred in the Balkans by drowning in the Danube, 315

17   Marianus, with presbyter Diodorus and others, martyred at Rome, 284

18   Hugo Gorovoka, native missionary at Miravovo,

Guadalcanal, in the Solomon Islands, 1918

21   Augurius and Eulogius, with bishop Fructuosus of
     Tarragoña, martyred by burning at the stake in Spain,
     259

22   Vincent of Saragossa, martyred at Valencia, Spain, 304

23   Parmenus, one of the seven ordained by the apostles
     (Acts 6:5), according to tradition martyred at Philippi
     in Macedonia, c. 98 [also July 28]

     Yona Kanamuzeni, martyr in Africa, 1964

24   Xenia (Eusebia), Kos, 5th c.

29   Caesarius, of Angoulême under its first bishop,
     Ausonius, 1st c.

## FEBRUARY

3    Celerinus, an African who suffered at Rome and was
     later ordained by Cyprian at Carthage, after 250

6    Luke, with bishop Silvanus of Emesa in Phoenicia,
     martyred after long imprisonment, 312

8    Stephen of Grandmont, hermit and founder of the
     (Benedictine) Grandmontines at Murat in France, 1124
     [He refused ordination as a priest to remain a deacon.]

9    Apollonia, martyred by fire at Alexandria, 249
     [Because her teeth were broken with pincers, she is the
     patron of dentists and toothache victims.]

     Primus and Donatus, slain by Donatist schismatics at
     Lavallum in northwest Africa, c. 297

12   Modestus, a native of Sardinia, martyred, c. 304.
     [His relics were brought to Benevento c. 785.]

14   Constantine (later Cyril), scholar, philologist, linguist,
     and (with his brother Methodius) missionary to the
     southern Slavs, 869

15   Joseph (Josippus) of Antioch, with seven others,
     martyred at Antioch, ?

21   Milnor Jones, missionary in western North Carolina,
     1916

23     Gorgonia, sister of Gregory Nazianzus
(The Theologian), c. 372

24     Flavian, with Montanus, Lucius, and their companions,
martyred at Carthage, 259

25     Elizabeth Fedde, pioneer Lutheran deaconess, 1921

28     Deacons of Alexandria, with presbyters and many
others, died ministering to the sick during the
plague, 262

## MARCH

8     Pontius, who attended Cyprian of Carthage in his exile
and at his trial and execution, and who wrote an account
of Cyprian's life and passion, c. 260

     Apollonius, of Antinoe in Egypt, with the actor
Philemon, cast into the sea at Alexandria, c. 305

12     Peter the Deacon, disciple, secretary, and companion of
Gregory the Great, after 605

14     Diaconus, of the church of the Marsi in central Italy,
martyred with two monks by the Lombards, 6th c.

16     Tatian, with bishop Hilary of Aquileia and others,
martyred by beheading, c. 284

18     Felix, with bishop Narcissus, martyrs at Gerona in
Spanish Catalonia, c. 307

19     Amantius, with presbyter Landoald, Romans sent by
the pope to evangelize what is now Belgium and
northeast France, c. 670

22     Octavian, archdeacon at Carthage, and several thousand
companions, martyred by Arians, 484

26     Irenaeus, with bishop Theodore of Pentapolis in Libya,
had his tongue cut out but survived and died in peace,
310

27     Pelagius, venerated at Treviso in Italy, ?

29     Cyril, martyred at Heliopolis, and companions, who
suffered under Julian the Apostate, c. 362

171
✳

31 Benjamin of Susa, with bishop Andos, martyred in
Persia, by torture for refusing to cease preaching
Christianity, c. 421

## APRIL

4 Agathopodes (Agathopus), with reader Theodulus,
martyred by drowning in Thessalonica for refusing to
give up the sacred books, 303

6 Platonida, founder of a nunnery at Nisibis in
Mesopotamia, 308

7 Rufinus, with Aquilina and their companions,
martyred in Sinope, ?

9 Elfgete, with abbot Theodore of Croyland and others,
put to death by the Danes, 870

10 Gajan, martyred in Dacia, ? 4th c.

13 Papylus, with bishop Carpus and others, martyred at
Pergamos, 150 (or 250)

16 Isabella Gilmore, deaconess, 1923

17 Peter, with his servant Hermogenes, martyred
probably at Antioch, ?

19 Timon, one of the seven ordained by the apostles
(Acts 6:5), 1st c. [also July 28]

21 Proculus, Sossius, and Faustus, with their bishop
Januarius and others, beheaded at Puteolum
(Campagna, central Italy), c. 305

22 Luke and Mucius, with companions, beheaded near
Babylon, c. 250

Abdiesus (Hebedjesus), one of a vast multitude
martyred in Persia, 341–380

Azadanes, martyred in Persia, 341–342

25 Philo and Agathopodes (Agathopus), who accompanied
Ignatius of Antioch to his martyrdom in Rome, brought
back his relics, and are believed to have written accounts
of his trial and death, c. 150

30 James, with reader Marianus and others, martyred at
Lambesa, an ancient town in Numidia (Algeria), 259

## MAY

1    Acius (Ache), with subdeacon Aceolus, martyred near Amiens, c. 303

2    Felix of Seville, martyred probably at Seville, ?

3    Diodorus and Rhodopianus, martyred in the province of Caria, Asia Minor, early 4th c.

4    Curcodomus, of Rome, who attended Peregrinus, first bishop of Auxerre, on a mission to Gaul, 3rd c.

5    Euthymius, martyred at Alexandria, ?

     Robert Pantutun, of Mota Island in the Banks Group in Vanuatu (formerly the New Hebrides), Melanesia, 1910

16   Sixteen Persian deacons (nine men and seven women), with bishop Audas (or Abdas) and seven presbyters, martyred in Persia, 420

19   Alcuin of York (Flaccus Albinus), abbot of Tours, 804

21   Timothy, Polius, and Eutychius, of the African province of Mauretania Caesariensis, martyred under Diocletian, ?

25   Winebald and Worad, of the abbey of St. Bertin, with companions, martyred by the Danes, 862

31   Paschasius, of Rome, author of some theological works that have become lost, c. 512

## JUNE

1    Valens, an aged deacon of Jerusalem, with Pamphilus and Porphyrius and companions, martyred at Caesarea in Palestine, 309

     Richard Henry Pemble, Archdeacon of Chicago, leader in the revival of the diaconate, 2001

2    Sanctus, one of the Martyrs of Lyons, 177

6    Ini Kopuria, founder of the Melanesian Brotherhood on Guadalcanal in the Solomon Islands, 1945

7    Wallabonsus, of Cordoba in Spain, with companions, beheaded for publicly rebuking Mohammed, 851

9    Vincent of Agen, martyred at Agen in Gascony for having disturbed a feast of the Gallic druids, ? c. 292

173

Ephraem the Syrian (Ephrem of Edessa), theologian and hymn-writer, 373

14  Anastasius, with Felix and Digna, martyred by beheading at Cordoba, 853

16  Ferrutio, with his brother the presbyter Ferreolus, natives of Asia Minor, sent by Irenaeus of Lyons to evangelize the country around Besançon, where they worked for 30 years and were then martyred, c. 212

Colman McRoi, disciple of Columba and abbot-founder of a monastery at Reachrain, now Lambay Island, Dublin, 6th c.

19  Culmatius, with bishop Gaudentius and others, martyred at Arezzo in Tuscany, 364

20  Demetrian, with presbyter Aristocleus and reader Athanasius, martyred at Cyprus, 305–311

27  Arialdus, persecuted and martyred by the party of the simoniac archbishop of Milan, 1066

✳ JULY

3  Irenaeus, with the noble lady Mustiola, martyred at Chiusi in Tuscany for having served other martyrs and buried their bodies, 273

5  Athanasius, martyred at Jerusalem for denouncing the heretic bishop, 452

15  Catulinus (Cartholinus), with companions, martyred at Carthage, ?

Gundisalvus Hendriquez, Portuguese deacon and Jesuit scholastic, 1570

19  Macrina the Younger, sister of Basil the Great and Gregory of Nyssa, 379

Arsenius the Great, of Rome, tutor to the emperor's sons and later hermit in the desert of Egypt, c. 449

20  Barhadbesciabas, of Arbela in Persia, martyred by beheading, 355

Paul of St. Zoilus, a community in Cordoba, Spain, imprisoned by the Muslims and beheaded, 851

25    Olympias of Constantinople, benefactor, cathedral staff
      member at Constantinople, and friend and disciple of the
      banished John Chrysostom, 410 [Also observed Dec. 17]

27    George, a monk from Palestine, with companions,
      martyred at Cordoba in Spain, c. 852.

28    Prochorus, Nicanor, Timon, Parmenus, and Nicolaus,
      companions of Stephen and Philip, 1st c. (see Acts 6:5)

      Irene Chrysobalantou, member of a community of
      women at Constantinople, 921

## AUGUST

5     Nonna of Nazianzus, evangelist, and educator within
      her family and the church, 374

7     Felicissimus, Agapitus, and four other deacons, with
      their bishop Sixtus II, beheaded at Rome, 258

8     Cyriacus, with companions, martyred at Rome, 304

10    Laurence of Rome, martyred at Rome, supposedly
      roasted on a gridiron but probably beheaded, 258

11    Euplus, racked and martyred in Catania of Sicily for
      having a copy of the gospels, 304

      Theodor, of the Monastery of the Caves near Kiev,
      martyred in 1088

13    Radegund of Poitiers, queen, hospital minister, then
      founder of Holy Cross convent at Poitiers, 587

16    Titus, put to death by a soldier during the sack of Rome
      by the Goths, while distributing alms to the poor,
      410 (or 426?)

17    Boniface, with companion monks in Africa, martyred
      by Arians, 483

      James the Deacon, Italian monk who accompanied
      Paulinus on his mission to Northumbria, 7th c.

20    Geert (Gerhard) Groote, founder of the Brethren of
      the Common Life, 1384

23    Archelaus, with bishop Quiriacus of Ostia and others,
      martyr, c. 234 (or 250?)

175

✳

25 Nemesius, with his daughter Lucilla, martyred at
Rome, c. 260

31 David Pendleton Oakerhater, former Cheyenne warrior,
missionary in Oklahoma, 1931

## SEPTEMBER

1 Ammon, with the Forty Holy Women, martyred in
Greece by placing a red-hot helmet on his head, c. 322

Laetus, with Vincent of Xaintes (first bishop of Dax
in Gascony), martyred, ? 5th c.

Hilaria, daughter of bishop Remigius of Rheims, 6th c.

3 Phoebe of Cenchreae (near Corinth), c. 64
(Romans 16:1-2)

7 Memorius, of Troyes, and companions, beheaded
by Attila, 451

15 Emilas, with Jeremiah, Spanish youths beheaded
at Cordoba, 852

16 Abundantius, beheaded at Rome, c. 303

19 Susanna, adult convert, martyred at Eleutheropolis, 362

20 Peter Rautamara and Edwin Nuagoro, first Papuan
deacons, 1914 (date of ordination)

23 Thekla, aged virgin, martyred at Iconium, late 1st c.

24 Thyrsus of Smyrna, with presbyter Andochius and
Felix, martyred in Gaul, 2nd c.

Anna E.B. Alexander, African American deaconess
and teacher in the diocese of Georgia, 1960

26 Thomas Clarkson, English campaigner for abolition
of slavery and the slave trade, 1846

## OCTOBER

1 Romanos Melodos, hymn-writer in Syria and
then Constantinople, c. 540

4 Francis of Assisi, 1226

5 Firmatus, with the virgin Flaviana, martyrs, venerated
at Auxerre in France, ?

8    Demetrius (Dimitri), martyred at Sirmium in Dalmatia, early 4th c.

     Ywe (Iwi, Ywi, Iwigius), of Northumbria, ordained by St. Cuthbert at Lindisfarne, hermit and miraculous healer in Brittany, relics at Wilton Abbey in England, d. 6 Oct. 690

9    Rusticus and Eleutherius, martyred at Paris with bishop Denis, c. 258

     Publia of Antioch, abbess and music minister at Antioch, c. 363

11   Philip the Deacon, one of the seven ordained by the apostles, 1st c. (Acts 6:5; 8:4–8, 26–40) [also observed June 6]

13   Papylas, with bishop Carpus, martyred at Pergamum, Asia Minor, 251

16   Baldwin (Balduinus, Baudoin), archdeacon at Laon, murdered, c. 680

20   Maximus of Aquila, martyred by being thrown from a cliff near his native city in southern Italy, c. 250

22   Severus, with bishop Philip of Heraclea, martyred by burning at the stake at Adrianopolis, for refusing to give up the sacred books, 304

24   Charles Sapibuana, of Gela or Nggela (called Florida by Spanish explorers), Melanesia, 1885

31   Nemesius, martyred in Rome, 3rd c.

## NOVEMBER

1    Caesarius the African, with presbyter Julian, martyred at Terracina, ?

3    Hilary, with presbyter Valentine, beheaded at Viterbo near Rome, c. 304

     Aeithalas, martyred in Persia, 379

10   Anianus, with bishop Demetrius and 21 companions, martyred at Antioch in Syria, ?

15   Abidus, of Edessa in Syria, martyred by burning, 322

17    Zachaeus, martyred by beheading at Caesarea
      in Palestine, 303

      Eugene, a disciple of Ambrose and deacon at
      Florence, 422

18    Romanos of Palestine, martyred at Antioch in Syria, 305

19    Faustus, companion in exile of Dionysius of Alexandria,
      martyred, 4th c.

29    Sisinius, sentenced to hard labor and later martyred
      at Rome, ? 309

## December

1     Nicholas Ferrar, founder of Little Gidding
      community, 1637

2     Marcellus, with companions, beheaded at
      Rome, 254–259

8     William West Skiles, farmer, missionary, and monk
      at Valle Crucis, North Carolina, 1862

10    Abundius, with presbyter Carpophorus, martyred
      at either Rome, Spoleto, or Seville, 290–300

15    Susanna, archimandrite, martyr, 3rd c. (perhaps
      identical to the Susanna listed at Sept. 19)

17    Awakrum or Abbacum of Serbia, ?

19    Timothy, burnt alive in Africa, c. 250

26    Stephen the Deacon, first martyr, c. 35 (Acts 6:1–7:3)

28    Domitian, with presbyter Eutychius, martyred at
      Ancyra in Galatia, ?

✳

## INTRODUCTION

1. Paulos Mar Gregorios, *The Meaning and Nature of Diakonia* (Geneva: World Council of Churches, 1988).

2. The three categories are outlined by John N. Collins, *Diakonia: Reinterpreting the Ancient Sources* (New York: Oxford University Press, 1990), 335–37, and expounded throughout his study.

3. Figaro and Susanna are the valet and maid in Mozart's *Le nozze di Figaro* (*The Marriage of Figaro*). Jeeves is Bertie Wooster's butler in the comic novels of P.G. Wodehouse. Bunter is Lord Peter Wimsey's manservant in the mystery novels of Dorothy Sayers. Dilsey is the long-suffering black servant in William Faulkner's *The Sound and the Fury*.

## CHAPTER I
## ORIGINS

1. For a general survey, see Lawrence R. Hennessey, "Diakonia and Diakonoi in the Pre-Nicene Church," in *Diakonia: Studies in Honor of Robert T. Meyer*, ed. Thomas Halton and Joseph P. Williams (Washington, D.C.: Catholic University of America Press, 1986), 60–86. For a major scholarly challenge, see Collins, *Diakonia*. Linking the biblical tradition to deacons, in two different ways, are James Monroe Barnett, *The Diaconate: A Full and Equal Order*, rev. ed. (Valley Forge, PA: Trinity Press International, 1995), 13–42, and John N. Collins, *Deacons and the Church: Making Connections between Old and New* (Harrisburg, PA: Morehouse Publishing, 2002), 27–85.

2. As noted by Deacon Maylanne Maybee of Toronto, at the bi-ennial NAAD conference on the diaconate, June 1989, *Diakoneo* 11, no. 4 (Sept. 1989): 1.

3. See Sr. Teresa, CSA, *Women in the Diaconate*, Distinctive Diaconate Studies 23 (1983–86), 1, no. 4. Sr. Teresa notes that a church at Cenchreae, a seaport of Corinth, is dedicated to St. Phoebe the Deacon. Her feast day in the Orthodox Church is September 3.

4. Throughout his gospel and Acts, Luke avoids using *diakonos*, a current title for Hermes and other messenger gods (Collins, *Diakonia*, 213).

## Chapter 2
## The Early Church

1. *Letter to the Corinthians* 49.6. Unless otherwise noted, patristic texts in this chapter are quoted from William A. Jurgens, ed., *The Faith of the Early Fathers*, 3 vols. (Collegeville, MN: Liturgical Press, 1970–79).

2. Barnett, Diaconate, 43–125; Hennessey, "Diakonia and Diakonoi in the Pre-Nicene Church," 74–86; Sr. Teresa, CSA, *Women in the Diaconate*; J. Robert Wright, "The Emergence of the Diaconate," *Liturgy: Diakonia* 2, no. 4 (fall 1982): 17–23, 67–71; and Edward P. Echlin, *The Deacon in the Church: Past and Future* (Staten Island, NY: Alba House, 1971), 14–94.

3. *Phil.* 4.1; *Trall.* 3.1 (see also *Magn.* 6.1, *Smyrn.* 12.2); *Trall.* 2.3.

4. From the Latin in H. Boone Porter Jr., *The Ordination Prayers of the Ancient Western Churches*, Alcuin Club Collections 49 (London: SPCK, 1967), 10.

5. See Sebastian Brock and Michael Vasey, ed., *The Liturgical Portions of the Didascalia*, Grove Liturgical Studies 29 (Bramcote, Notts.: Grove Books, 1982), 11–12, 15–16, 22–23. See also Robert Nowell, *The Ministry of Service: Deacons in the Contemporary Church* (New York: Herder and Herder, 1968), 24–29.

6. Sr. Teresa, CSA, e-mail to author, 6 Feb. 2004.

7. Ambrose, *De Off.* I.41.214. The reference to "consecration" means at least administration of the wine—but perhaps more.

8. From AC 8.17–20 in Franz Xaver von Funk, ed., *Didascalia et Constitutiones apostolorum*, 2 vols. (Paderborn: Schoeningh, 1905), 1:522–25. For a recent English translation, see W. Jardine Grisbrooke, ed., *The Liturgical Portions of the Apostolic Constitutions:*

*A Text for Students,* The Alcuin Club and the Group for Renewal of Worship, Joint Liturgical Studies 13–14 (Bramcote, Notts.: Grove Books, 1990), 75–76.

9. See John St. H. Gibaut, *The Cursus Honorum: A Study of the Origins and Evolution of Sequential Ordination* (New York: Peter Lang, 2000), and John St. H. Gibaut, *Sequential or Direct Ordination? A Return to the Sources,* The Alcuin Club and the Group for Renewal of Worship, Joint Liturgical Studies 55 (Cambridge, U.K.: Grove Books, 2003).

10. Translation of Canon 19 by Sr. Teresa, *Women in the Diaconate,* 2:34.

## CHAPTER 3
## EPISCOPAL CHURCH: EARLY DEACONS

1. The concept of the four waves was proposed by James L. Lowery Jr. in 1979. I have changed his order to put missionary deacons first, since they were the earliest in terms of ordination dates and canonical provision.

2. See Susan Fenimore Cooper, *William West Skiles, a Sketch of Missionary Life at Valle Crucis in Western North Carolina 1841–1862* (n.p., 1890).

3. See *Oakerhater* (Oklahoma City: St. John's Episcopal Church Press, 1982), and Lois Clark, *David Pendleton Oakerhater: God's Warrior* (Oklahoma City: Diocese of Oklahoma, 1985).

4. See Owanah Anderson, *Jamestown Commitment. The Episcopal Church and the American Indian* (Cincinnati: Forward Movement Publications, 1988), 56, 68, 70–71, 79–80, 109, 128.

5. For the English history, see Janet Grierson, *The Deaconess* (London: CIO, 1981).

6. Mary P. Truesdell, "The Office of Deaconess," in *The Diaconate Now,* ed. Richard T. Nolan, (Washington, DC: Corpus Books, 1968), 158–61.

7. *EWHP Newsletter* 4, no. 1 (winter 1984): 1; 7, no. 4 (fall 1987): 1; 8, no. 1 (winter 1988): 7–8. In 1978 the National Center for the Diaconate formed the Deaconess History Project, directed by Kathryn A. Piccard. The project consisted of three parts: a directory of the 450 deaconesses, an archive of deaconess books and

other material, and an oral history project, with taped interviews of deaconesses by Piccard and Mary Sudman Donovan, whose book *A Different Call: Women's Ministries in the Episcopal Church, 1850–1920* (Wilton, CT: Morehouse-Barlow, 1986), contains information about Episcopal deaconesses.

8. *EWHP Newsletter* 3, no. 4 (fall 1984): 6.

9. *EWHP Newsletter* 5, no. 4 (fall 1985): 3; 6, no. 1 (winter 1986): 8.

10. "Deaconess Harriet Bedell: Missionary to the Mikasukis," *The Diocesan* [Diocese of Florida] (Advent 1989): 9.

11. Material on Nevada deaconesses furnished by Josephine Borgeson. See *Diakoneo* 12, no. 3 (May 1990).

12. Robert E. Gard, *The Deacon* (Madison, WI: R. Bruce Allison Wisconsin Books, 1979).

CHAPTER 4
EPISCOPAL CHURCH: CONTEMPORARY DEACONS

1. The stories in this chapter are drawn from personal correspondence, and I thank the writers for permission to quote from their letters and e-mail messages.

2. "Proceedings: The Diaconate" (Papers delivered at Conference on the Diaconate, Notre Dame, IN, 1979), mimeographed (Boston: National Center for the Diaconate, 1979), and "Summary and Selected Proceedings: Second National Conference on the Diaconate, May 21–23, 1981," mimeographed (Boston: National Center for the Diaconate, 1981). For the major papers delivered at the three conferences, see J. Robert Wright, "The Emergence of the Diaconate," *Liturgy: Diakonia* 2, no. 4 (fall 1982): 17–23, 67–71; John E. Booty, "The Church as Servant," *Open* (Oct. 1981): 4–10; and Durstan R. McDonald, "Thoughts on the Diaconate," *Open* (Oct. 1984): 6–15.

3. Browning's speech and the dialogue on the transitional diaconate are printed in *Diakoneo* 9, no. 2 (summer 1987): 2–7, 13–15.

4. *Open* (June 1977): 1.

5. *Diakoneo* 11, no. 5 (Nov. 1989): 1–2.

CHAPTER 5
OTHER CHURCHES

1. Wilhelm Schamoni's notes (now lost) were expanded in his *Familienvater als geweihte Diakone* (Paderborn: Schoeningh, 1953), published in English as *Married Men as Ordained Deacons* (London: Burns and Oates, 1955). See Joseph Hornef and Paul Winninger, "Chronique de la restauration du diaconat (1945–1965)," in *Le diacre dans l'Église et le monde d'aujourd'hui*, ed. Paul Winninger and Yves Congar (Paris: Les Éditions du Cerf, 1966), 205–6.

2. *Council Speeches of Vatican II*, ed. Hans Küng, Yves Congar, and Daniel O'Hanlon (Glen Rock, NJ: Paulist Press, 1964), 103–4.

3. Patrick McCaslin and Michael G. Lawler, *Sacrament of Service: A Vision of the Permanent Diaconate Today* (New York: Paulist Press, 1986), 88.

4. For a critical discussion of this problem, see Sherri L. Wallace, "The Restoration of the Permanent Diaconate: A Blending of Roles," *Worship* 77, no. 6 (Nov. 2003): 530–52.

5. Lambeth Conference 1958, *The Encyclical Letter from the Bishops together with the Resolutions and Reports* (London: SPCK, 1958), 1:50, 2:106–7. In addition to "distinctive," the committee report used the term "permanent diaconate."

6. Bishop of St. Andrews [John Howe], "The Diaconate," in Lambeth Conference 1968, *Preparatory Essays* (London: SPCK, 1968), 62–74.

7. Lambeth Conference 1968, *Resolutions and Reports* (London: SPCK; Greenwich, CT: Seabury Press, 1968), 38–39. For the full text, see the Appendix.

8. Lambeth Conference 1978, *The Report of the Lambeth Conference 1978* (London: CIO, [1978]), 44. See also p. 81 and James B. Simpson and Edward M. Story, *Discerning God's Will: The Complete Eyewitness Report of the Eleventh Lambeth Conference* (Nashville: Thomas Nelson Publishers, 1979), 307.

9. ACC-3 (Report of Third Meeting: Trinidad 1976) (London: Anglican Consultative Council, 1976), 42.

10. *The Truth Shall Make You Free: The Lambeth Conference 1988, The Reports, Resolutions and Pastoral Letters from the Bishops* (London:

Church House Publishing, for Anglican Consultative Council, 1988), 55–56.

11. *Diakoneo* 20, no. 4 (fall/winter 1998): 1, 5. At later celebrations during Lambeth 1998, an English deacon and an Australian deaconess served at the Eucharist.

12. *Deacons in the Ministry of the Church: A Report to the House of Bishops of the General Synod of the Church of England*, GS 802 (London: Church House Publishing, 1988).

13. *Distinctive Diaconate News* 24 (Sept. 1989): 1.

14. These publications may be ordered from sister.teresa@london.anglican.org.

15. Reginald H. Fuller, "An Anglican Odyssey, 1987–88," *Open* (Dec. 1988): 3.

16. Sources on the diaconate in the Anglican Communion include Bavin, 43–50; Sr. Teresa, "An Anglican Perspective on the Diaconate—1988," Distinctive Diaconate Study 29 (1988): 17–19; numerous issues of *Distinctive Diaconate News*; and *Diakoneo* 10, no. 5 (Nov. 1988): 2; 11, no. 4 (Sept. 1989): 5. Sr. Teresa also read this chapter and made many suggestions.

17. *A New Zealand Prayer Book, He Karakia Mihinare o Aotearoa* (Auckland: William Collins Publishers Ltd., 1989), 897. Except for a few phrases, the ordination prayers for bishops and priests are similar to the prayer for deacons.

18. *Baptism, Eucharist and Ministry* (Geneva: World Council of Churches, 1982), 27. A summary of official responses from the churches, on deacons and the diaconate, appears in *Diakoneo* 10, no. 3 (May 1988) through 12, no. 1 (Jan. 1990).

19. *Diakoneo* 12, no. 1 (Jan. 1990): 10.

20. Kyriaki Karidoyanes Fitzgerald, *Women Deacons in the Orthodox Church: Called to Holiness and Ministry* (Brookline, MA: Holy Cross Orthodox Press, 1998).

21. See Dick Pemble, "The Diaconate and Called to Mission," *Diakoneo* 22, no. 3 (Pentecost 2000): 3, 12–13.

22. *The Diaconate as Ecumenical Opportunity*, The Hanover Report of the Anglican-Lutheran International Commission (London: Anglican Communion Publications, 1996).

23. *Distinctive Diaconate News* 23 (March 1989): 7.

## CHAPTER 6
## THE FINDING, NURTURE, AND CARE OF DEACONS

1. The Title III canons on ministry are available online at http://www.episcopalchurch.org. See also the commentaries on the 2003 canons by Ormonde Plater and Ted Nitz, *Diakoneo* 25, no. 6 (Advent 2003): 12–16, which I have adapted for this chapter.

2. In Northern Michigan in 1990, Bishop Thomas K. Ray began to commission, in a single liturgy, "ministry support teams" in small parishes. Each team includes [lay] coordinators of ministry, local priests, and local deacons. See *The Living Church* (27 May 1990): 8.

3. The Ordination of a Bishop, Book of Common Prayer (1979), 518.

4. Book of Common Prayer (1979), 13.

5. See Ormonde Plater, *Deacons in the Liturgy* (Harrisburg, PA: Morehouse Publishing, 1992), and Howard E. Galley, *The Ceremonies of the Eucharist: A Guide to Celebration* (Cambridge, MA: Cowley Publications, 1989).

6. Galley, 28, discourages the practice of priests vesting and performing the role of deacon as unfaithful to the prayer book rubrics (BCP, 354). Also opposed is Byron D. Stuhlman, *Prayer Book Rubrics Expanded* (New York: Church Hymnal Corp., 1987), 15. See also Dennis G. Michno, *A Priest's Handbook: The Ceremonies of the Church*, 3rd ed. (Harrisburg, PA: Morehouse Publishing, 1998), 78, and the Roman Catholic *Ceremonial of Bishops* (Collegeville, MN: Liturgical Press, 1986), 22.

## CHAPTER 7
## THE ORDINATION OF DEACONS

1. For a summary of Anglican thought on bishops, see Richard A. Norris, "Episcopacy," in *The Study of Anglicanism*, ed. Stephen Sykes and John Booty (London: SPCK; Philadelphia: Fortress Press, 1988), 296–309.

2. For a summary of Anglican thought on priests, see John B. Webster, "Ministry and Priesthood," in ibid., 285–90.

3. For extended definitions of the diaconate, see *Deacons in the Ministry of the Church*, 77–99; Anglican Church of Canada,

Committee on Ministry, *A Plan to Restore the Diaconate in the Anglican Church of Canada* (Toronto: Anglican Church of Canada, 1989), 4–8; and Sr. Teresa, CSA, "An Anglican Perspective on the Diaconate," *Distinctive Diaconate Study* 29 (1988).

4. BCP, including italics: "My brother."

5. *A Greek-English Lexicon of the New Testament and other Early Christian Literature*, 3rd ed., rev. and ed. Frederick William Danker (Chicago: University of Chicago Press, 2000).

6. Aidan Kavanagh, *Elements of Rite: A Handbook of Liturgical Style* (New York: Pueblo Publishing Co., 1982), 76.

7. Ibid., 32.

8. Hymns 502 or 504, 503, and 226 in *The Hymnal 1982*; No. 832 (a Taizé chant) in *Wonder, Love, and Praise*.

9. Gail Ramshaw, "Formation in Prayer and Worship: Living the Eucharistic Prayer," in *The Baptismal Mystery and the Catechumenate*, ed. Michael W. Merriman (New York: Church Hymnal Corp., 1990), 73.

## CHAPTER 8
### DEACONS AND THEIR STORIES

1. At my invitation, the twenty-five deacons contributed their stories by e-mail, with permission to publish, and I edited them for this chapter.

2. Budgerigar, an Australian parakeet popular in Great Britain and, presumably, its former colonies.

## CHAPTER 9
### PASCHAL DEACONS IN A PASCHAL CHURCH

1. Parts of this chapter are adapted, by permission, from Ormonde Plater, "The Four Faces of the Diaconate," *Diakoneo* 18, no. 4 (Michaelmas 1996): 3–4; 18, no. 5 (All Saints 1996): 4; 19, no. 1 (Epiphany 1997): 6; and 19, no. 2 (Lent 1997): 7. © The North American Association for the Diaconate, Inc.

2. Reprinted, by permission, from Ormonde Plater, "Exsultet," *The Living Church*, 15 April 1990, 13. © The Living Church Foundation, Inc.

✳

I n addition to printed material, those studying the diaconate in Anglican churches are invited to use two electronic resources: www.diakonoi.org, the website of the North American Association for the Diaconate (with links to other deacon sites), and the Internet list Anglodeacons, which can be joined through groups.yahoo.com.

Arnold, Kenneth. *On the Way: Vocation, Awareness, and Fly Fishing.* New York: Church Publishing Inc., 2000.

Barnett, James Monroe. *The Diaconate: A Full and Equal Order.* Rev. ed. Valley Forge, PA: Trinity Press International, 1995.

Booty, John E. *The Servant Church: Diaconal Ministry and the Episcopal Church.* Wilton, CT: Morehouse-Barlow, 1982.

Borgeson, Josephine, and Lynne Wilson, eds. *Reshaping Ministry: Essays in Memory of Wesley Frensdorff.* Arvada, CO: Jethro Publications, 1990.

Collins, John N. *Diakonia: Reinterpreting the Ancient Sources.* New York: Oxford University Press, 1990.

———. *Are All Christians Ministers?* Collegeville, MN: Liturgical Press, 1992.

———. *Deacons and the Church: Making Connections between Old and New.* Harrisburg, PA: Morehouse Publishing, 2003.

Cummings, Owen F. *Deacons and the Church.* New York: Paulist Press, 2004.

*Diakoneo.* Newsletter of the North American Association for the Diaconate, 1978–.

✳

*Directory of Deacons.* Providence, RI: North American Association for the Diaconate, annual.

*Distinctive Diaconate News.* Edited by Sr. Teresa, CSA. Newsletter of Distinctive Diaconate, London, 1981–.

*Distinctive Diaconate Studies.* Edited by Sr. Teresa, CSA. Occasional papers of Distinctive Diaconate, London, 1981–1989.

Ditewig, William T. *101 Questions and Answers on Deacons.* New York: Paulist Press, 2004.

Gibaut, John St. H. *The Cursus Honorum: A Study of the Origins and Evolution of Sequential Ordination.* New York: Peter Lang, 2000.

———. *Sequential or Direct Ordination? A Return to the Sources.* Alcuin Club and Group for Renewal of Worship, Joint Liturgical Studies 55. Cambridge, England: Grove Books, 2003.

Gregorios, Paulos Mar. *The Meaning and Nature of Diakonia.* Geneva: WCC, 1988.

Hallenbeck, Edwin F., ed. *The Orders of Ministry: Reflections on Direct Ordination.* Providence, RI: North American Association for the Diaconate, 1996.

Halton, Thomas, and Joseph P. Williman, ed. *Diakonia: Studies in Honor of Robert T. Meyer.* Washington, DC: Catholic University of America Press, 1986.

Hartley, Ben L., and Paul E. Van Buren. *The Deacon: Ministry Through Words of Faith and Acts of Love.* Nashville: United Methodist Church, 1999.

International Theological Commission [Roman Catholic]. *From the Diakonia of Christ to the Diakonia of the Apostles.* Chicago: Liturgy Training Publications, 2004.

*Liturgy: Diakonia.* Journal of the Liturgical Conference 2, no. 4 (Fall 1982).

Marshall, Paul V., and Lesley A. Northrup, ed. *Leaps and Boundaries: The Prayer Book in the 21st Century.* Harrisburg, PA: Morehouse Publishing, 1997.

McCaslin, Patrick, and Michael G. Lawler. *Sacrament of Service. A Vision of the Permanent Diaconate Today.* New York: Paulist Press, 1986.

Mullan, David S. *Diakonia and the Moa.* Auckland, New Zealand: Methodist Theological College, 1984.

Plater, Ormonde. *Many Servants: An Introduction to Deacons.* Boston: Cowley Publications, 1991.

———. *Deacons in the Liturgy.* Harrisburg, PA: Morehouse Publishing, 1992.

———. *The Passion Gospels of Matthew, Mark, Luke and John from the New Revised Standard Version set to traditional chant.* New York: Church Hymnal Corp., 1992.

———. *Intercession: A Theological and Practical Guide.* Boston: Cowley Publications, 1995.

Shugrue, Timothy J. *Service Ministry of the Deacon.* Washington, DC: United States Catholic Conference, 1988.

Sr. Teresa, CSA. *Women in the Diaconate.* Distinctive Diaconate Studies 23. London: Community of St. Andrew, 1983–86.

Slocum, Robert Boak. *A New Conversation: Essays on the Future of Theology and the Episcopal Church.* New York: Church Publishing Inc., 1999.

Sprague, Minka. *Praying from the Free-Throw Line—for Now.* New York: Church Publishing Inc., 1999.

Wood, Susan K. *Sacramental Orders.* Collegeville, MN: Liturgical Press, 2000.

✳

✳

✳